# In Days Gone B

## A History of Stockton on the
## North Yorkshire

© The Stockton on the Forest & Hopgrove Local History Group

Pamela Richards Publications - July 2011

ISBN 978-0-9558822-4-1

Editor: Bobby Hughes
Assistant Editors: Tiz Bacon, Joy Moseley

Digital Archive: Simon Moseley
Design & Artwork: Peter Bacon

Printed by The Max Design & Print Co
Chessingham Park, Common Road, Dunnington, York  YO19 5SE

*This book is dedicated to the memory of*
*Terry Cooper*
*an enthusiastic historian and founder member*
*who proved an inspiration to many of us*

# *Acknowledgements*

*The History Group wishes to thank all donors and lenders of photographs, drawings and other memorabilia which have been used in this book and also donated over a period of years to the club archives. We also acknowledge all those who have helped in any way with the production of the book, most particularly the chapter authors who have willingly and enthusiastically searched their own records and memories to contribute to the text.*

*We particularly wish to thank the staff of the Borthwick Institute, York Reference Library, York Archives, and the County Library at Northallerton for their help and assistance.*

*Similarly we are indebted to our church wardens for their help in our researches, the management of the School, Stockton Hall, the village Methodist fraternity, the Village Hall Management Committee and Dean's Garden Centre for their interest and contributions. Equally our thanks to the several village groups and societies who have been so keen to help.*

*Finally the History Group wishes to record grateful thanks to the production team for their hard work, commitment and perseverance.*

# Contents

| Chapter | | Author | Page |
|---|---|---|---|
| Foreword | | Terry Briggs | iv |
| 1 | Back To The Beginning | Steve Burton | 1 |
| 2 | The Shape Of Things To Come | Malcolm Jennings | 6 |
| 3 | From Stoc Tun to Stockton | Malcolm Jennings | 11 |
| 4 | Who Goes There? | John Strong | 14 |
| 5 | Stockton Rifles | John Strong | 20 |
| 6 | Stockton Hall | Steve Burton | 23 |
| 7 | The Village & Monuments | Steve Burton | 25 |
| 8 | Holy Trinity Church | Bobby Hughes | 30 |
| 9 | The Chapel | Maureen Sutcliffe, Madeline Jilbert, Lily Dunn, Joan Rawkins, Betty Willis | 36 |
| 10 | The Bull Centre | Frances Beattie | 41 |
| 11 | Wellies & Watering Cans | Imogen Walker | 42 |
| 12 | The Yorkshire Herald | — | 46 |
| 13 | First Class Service | Joy Garvie | 48 |
| 14 | Open All Hours | Angela Piercy | 51 |
| 15 | Sup Up Lads! | Terry Briggs | 53 |
| 16 | From Hut To Hall | Terry Briggs | 57 |
| 17 | Pen, Ink & Blots | Maureen Sutcliffe, Joan Rawkins | 59 |
| 18 | Carnival Time | Jill Hawkins | 64 |
| 19 | Three Cheers For The WI | Barbara Hardisty | 71 |
| 20 | Treading The Boards | Pat Jennings | 76 |
| 21 | Musical Folk | Jim Boldry | 80 |
| 22 | Sporting Times | Noel Marshall | 83 |
| 23 | Tally Ho! | Terry Briggs | 87 |
| 24 | All Change! | John Strong | 89 |
| 25 | Duckhams & Swanns | Frank Swann, Terry Briggs | 96 |
| 26 | History In The Making | — | 98 |

# Foreword

*Our History Group has been in existence for four years. One of our original objectives was to collect and store village memorabilia; photographs, maps, family trees, military history and building records. In fact, we collected any document which illustrated the lives of our forefathers. We also recorded interviews on tape given by some of our more senior village personalities as they recalled their early days. These were later transcribed into written records.*

*Our endeavours have been very successful. We have been well received during our research and we take great satisfaction in preserving the knowledge and experiences learned in the past and in making them available for future generations.*

*Our decision to produce a village book allowed us to widen the scope and range of our contributors even further. We have been delighted by their interest and assistance.*

*We hope you enjoy 'In Days Gone By' - a little dip into the history of Stockton on the Forest and that you will embrace the past with enthusiasm. Surrounded as we are by change and development, history gives us an understanding of our place in the world, what this area used to be like and how it has developed into the village we know today.*

*Terry Briggs - Chairman*

# Chapter 1

# *Back To The Beginning*

Thousands of years after the Great Ice Age a gradual thaw occurred which resulted in a huge inland sea covering the vast area of what is now the Vale of York surrounded by the Dales, Moors and Wolds. As the waters subsided, drainage rivers from these hills began carving their way through the deposits which had accumulated. Great moraines – huge walls of debris - had been pushed along in front of the Ice Age glaciers, with smaller side moraines running in a north/south line between the rivers Derwent and Foss. It eventually became a densely forested landscape on the eastern edge of the mighty Forest of Galtres. This raised ridge of scoured cobbles, large and small, became a natural feature which could be followed, prior to Roman times, northwards from the developing settlement of York to Malton and the North York Moors.

## *Were the Romans here in Stockton?*

The Roman settlement of *Derventium* (Malton) developed shortly after the fortified town of *Eboracum* (York) which was built around 70 AD. It had huge stone walls and massive stone buildings and was known as 'The Rome of the North'. *Eboracum* lasted 250 years or so until the collapse of the Roman Empire. It was the Empire's most northern permanently manned fortress. Constantine (later The Great) was proclaimed Emperor there in 304 AD. The city was re-named *Eforwick* under Saxon rule, then *Jorvik* by the Vikings and ultimately York, following the Norman Conquest.

The road connecting *Eboracum* to *Derventium* is widely believed to have followed the ridge of higher ground which ran through our village. Such a road would have been constructed out of small rocks laid along the top of the ridge to prevent erosion by animal hooves, wagons and marching feet. Although no remaining surface is visible, cobbles used as foundations in early 18th century properties are believed to have been salvaged from this road. Evidence of Roman habitation can be found in the parish as the possible site of a Roman villa is currently being investigated.

Following the Romans' departure, a local populace of Brigantines is believed to have cleared areas of forest for agricultural purposes. Over the centuries they would have fought and ultimately settled with the invaders of these shores – the Angles, Saxons and Vikings. In the 11th century, a mainly Saxon community developed calling the village 'Stocca' or 'Stocthun' roughly translated as Stockade in the Forest. One can imagine a defensive wooden stockade surrounding a community living in the forest on the edge of the Roman road. More hamlets existed at Carleton and Sandburn.

# The Norman Conquest

No doubt the area would have seen much violence at the time of the Norman Conquest. Shortly before the Battle of Hastings, King Hadrada the Viking invaded the North of England in a final bid to seize control from the Saxons. The northern Earls loyal to King Harold raised an army of fighting men from around York in their bid to stop the city from falling to Hadrada. They were, however, defeated at the Battle of Fulford, south of the city. This defeat resulted in Harold force-marching his army from the south coast where they had been awaiting the Norman Duke William's invasion. Having arrived in the north, Harold's forces skirted around the city and tricked the Vikings, who had been joined by Harold's own brother Tostig, forcing them into a battle at Stamford Bridge. It is possible that the remnants of the northern Earls' army may have joined up with Harold using the road through Stockton, which joins the Stamford Bridge road from York. With the element of surprise, Harold split the Viking forces and vanquished their exhausted reinforcements who were camped with their long-ships at Cawood, near Naburn. However, news broke of William's imminent landing. Harold marched south with battle weary troops to face the Normans outside Hastings at Senlac Hill where he was defeated. The men of Yorkshire were far from happy with their new Norman masters. Tension and unrest soon led to outbreaks of violence which King William quelled by sending his troops to carry out what became known as 'the harrying of the north'. The rebels were poorly organised as no leader had emerged to champion their rebellion, unlike Hereward the Wake who was notorious for his defence of the Fens. William's nobles subdued the uprisings, razing villages to the ground, forcing people to scatter into the forests and poisoning their fields with salt which made them infertile for years. This action was responsible for the derivation of the word 'waste' which appeared in the country's first Register of Property.

# The Domesday Book

William the Conqueror carried out a survey of the whole kingdom to record in minute detail the names of those who owned land and its condition. The Saxons forfeited much of their property in reprisal for supporting the rebellion against William's forces. Land remaining in Saxon hands was subject to much dispute. The survey highlighted which land belonged to the crown and which to the church, stating the income due to each. The entire Domesday Book was written by one scribe in a stylised and abbreviated form of 11th century clerical Latin.

The entry for Stockton on the Forest reads:

*'In Stocheton ad gld . 111. carucates.um.den 11.car poll.ee. Com.A.he.waft'.e.'*
In Stockton on the Forest [are] three carucates to the geld and there could be two ploughs. Count Alan has it and it is waste.

*Gld:* Geldrun: A periodic tax (Danegeld) first raised for the Danish wars (Vikings) at a number of pence per hide, carucates or solung.

*Carucate:* Carucate, carucata, carrucata: Measurement of land in the Danish counties, the equivalent of a hide. Used in Domesday for tax purposes.

*Poll:* Plough: Caruca, carruca. In Domesday the word implies a plough team with its eight oxen and the plough itself. The measure of a carucate was originally the amount of land which such a team could plough in one day.

*Com.A:* Count Alan. He was granted many areas of land in twelve counties of England as one of William's strong supporters. These lands were passed to Thomas de Normanvill in 1092. By 1303 Peter de Mauley had inherited 2 carucates. The over-lordship of the manor was ascribed to the de Mauley heirs two centuries later but probably fell into abeyance not long afterwards. In 1292 the whole three carucates were subinfeudated to Gaceus de Chaumont, mayor of York in 1256. At his death they passed to his 18 month old son John. He died in 1316, being the only landowner 'returned' for the parish.

*Waft:* Waste: Land which was either unusable or uncultivated and not taxed.
Although waste was sometimes the result of William's wars in the north, it could also mean land not fit for agricultural use. Much of the land in the East Riding especially did not return to its former fertility for over 100 years.


# The Middle Ages

John Chaumont filled many important offices in Yorkshire during the mid 14th century. When Sir John Chaumont died in 1373 his heir was placed by the King under the guardianship of Brian Stapleton. This ensured that ownership of the de Chaumont family was carried forward, although they were unable to retain the whole of their lands in future years.

In 1388/9 John Chaumont's manor of Stockton on the Moor was settled on his daughter Margaret and her husband William Mowbray. Should they die childless, Elizabeth (daughter of William's younger brother Alexander) and her husband William Gascoigne would inherit. William and Margaret's daughter Eleanor became wife of Thomas Ingleby, Lord of Ripley and East Harlsey. In 1564 Sir William Ingleby and his wife Anne sold land in Stockton to Anthony Bayock. Nineteen years later Anthony and Alice Bayock together with Thomas and Anne Elwood conveyed the manor of Stockton to George Stable. George and his wife Dorothy held lands in the parish in 1590. Later the manor seems to have passed to the descendants of Lawrence Agar, a local landowner, until his death in 1583.

## Sandburn

From 1086 three carucates in this parish known as Sandburn (Sanbura XI cent; Santburn X11 cent) were then in the possession of Ralph Paynel, but were claimed by the canons of York as having been theirs under the Confessor. Before 1159 the canons recovered part of the land and granted it to Rievaulx Abbey which had owned tenements here since the 16th century, valued annually at £1 16s. In 1270 Henry III granted Thomas de Bolton the 'lawns' of Carlton and Sandburn in the Forest of Galtres, then valued at 40s a year. Thomas was allowed to surround them with a dyke and a hedge low enough to allow the deer to come in and out. It was, no doubt, in consequence of this grant that both 'lawns' were soon afterwards brought into cultivation and their tithes assigned by the archbishop in 1272 to the chapel of Stockton.


## Carlton

Three geld carucates in Carlton (Carletone xi. Cent: Carleton, Karleton, xiv. Cent) belonging to the see of York in 1086 were included in the King's gift to Thomas de Bolton and descended with Sandburn until their acquisition in the 16th century by Lawrence Agar. Before his death in 1583 he made a settlement of his grange of Carlton and the lands belonging to him, to his wife Agnes and his younger son John. In the possession of John Agar, who held them after his mother's death, they were probably united into the manor of Stockton in the late 1700s.

# The Agar connection

Lawrence Agar's younger son John died in 1636 leaving a son of the same name. By his second wife, Isabel Gibson, this John was father of a third John Agar, Lord of the manors of Stockton and Holtby from 1679.

In 1673 the Hearth Tax List shows Jo (John) Agar having 6 hearths in the Bulmer Wapentake District.

## HEARTH TAX LIST 1673 – BULMER WAPENTAKE

| | | | |
|---|---|---|---|
| Jo Agar  6 | Ch.Pick  1 | Ja Wilkinson 3 | Jo Lazenby  1 |
| Steph. Wilkinson 1 | Tho Lazenby 1 | Jno West 1 | Jo Cooper 1 |
| Wm. Wikinson 1 | Rd Lazenby 2 | Jo Lound 1 | Math Lazenby 1 |
| Tho. Goonseyer 1 | Rbt Amerson 1 | Rich Leefe 1 | Tho West 2 |
| Jae Wilkinson 1 | Rbt Broughton 1 | Robt Wilton 1 | Fran Agar 1 |
| Jo Rudsdyke 1 | Marg Wilkinson 1 | Jo Burland 2 | Robt Rook 1 |
| Tho Waude 2 | Rd Ridsdale 1 | Tho Watkins 2 | Will Wood 1 |
| Geo Wilkinson 2 | Jo Rushton 1 | Wlt West 1 | John Beales 1 |
| Jo Ulewman  1 | Bryan Richardson 1 | Geo Thompson 2 | Andrew Bulmer 1 |
| Thos Lazenby Jnr. 1 | Jo Wilkinson 1 | | |

The Hearth Tax was a highly unpopular tax introduced after the Restoration of the Monarchy and was repealed in 1689 when William and Mary came to the throne. The rate was two shillings per annum payable in equal parts on Lady Day and Michaelmas. Inevitably there was evidence of widespread tax evasion.

The manors of Stockton and Carlton were in the hands of the Agar family and they are believed to have had a manor house where Trinity Meadows now stands (reference an early 20th century map showing a manor house on that site). A further John Agar passed the manor house to his sisters Margaret Agar, Mary Foord and Elizabeth Wilson on his death in 1754. Margaret Agar died unmarried in 1762 leaving her share to her nephew Thomas Wilson and then to his children before it was passed to another nephew Thomas Preston. Mary Foord left her share directly to Benjamin Preston, son of Thomas Preston, stipulating that he must take up the Agar name and coat of arms, which he duly did in 1786 after Mary's death. Elizabeth Wilson's share however appears to have descended via her son Thomas to Elizabeth Cooper (presumably Thomas' daughter) who married Rev John Ware, Incumbent of Holy Trinity in the year 1791 (the third appointee in that year) and later of the Stockton Rifles fame. A division of the estate took place in 1802 between Benjamin Preston Agar and Elizabeth Cooper Ware in which Stockton Hall (the manor house) passed to Mrs Ware. Shortly afterwards Benjamin commenced building Brockfield Hall as his residence using Peter Atkinson of York as architect. The building and fitting took until 1824 to complete at a cost of £8,239 6s 3d.

Rev Ware claimed that £107 15s worth of repairs were needed for Stockton Hall including two ranges to dining and drawing room, ranges in the kitchen and servants quarters and two lead cisterns. Benjamin produced testimonials to prove the house was in a better state of repair than when he had taken it over. Indeed records indicate that in 1793 he had spent £758 5s 6d on repairs. The Agars moved to Brockfield Hall, completed about 1807 when the house was considered habitable, retaining their title of lords of the manor. Rev Ware died in the early part of the 1800s, his estate passing to his wife Elizabeth and eventually to her three sons. One son, Henry, became a lawyer joining with John Brook in legal partnership. The practice eventually became known as Innes Ware until 1966, finally becoming Ware & Co which operates to this day. It is apparent from the enclosure maps of 1815 that Mrs Cooper Ware held a great deal of land in the village mainly between the church and the prayer tree. This included the area believed to be the site of the manor house.

Benjamin Agar died in 1852 and after the death of his son in 1871, Brockfield Hall passed to Harriet Agar. She died in 1904 and the estate was left to William Talbot Agar but despite his surname it is not clear what relation he was, if any. The estate was sold in 1923 by his son Charles to Mrs Mary Ellison and two years later to Mr Herbert Murgatroyd. In 1951 it was bought by Lord and Lady Martin Fitzalan.

## *The 18th and 19th Centuries*

It was during the early part of the 18th century that the 'modern' village started to take shape mainly on either side of the main street; the forerunner of the 'linear village' it remains to this day. Many properties were built for farm workers, tradespeople and shepherds etc. who worked on the Agar Estate. Eventually these were passed on by marriage settlements and inheritance. Towards the end of this century the village stretched from the prayer tree at the York end to the blacksmith's at Carr Bank Lane as shown on the 1815 Enclosure Act map. This map shows no Stockton Hall on the present day site but does show the land in the possession of Hall Plummer who had lived in East Lilling in 1774 and at Bilton Hall in 1801. His address in 1814 was recorded as Stockton Hall, suggesting it was he who built the hall we recognise today. His family lived there until the death of his daughter Harriet in 1834, when it was sold to the Lloyd family.

By now the village had assumed its present day core shape made up of farms, workers cottages, two public houses, various business units and shops. These are more fully described in the chapters relating to specific buildings.

## *The 20th Century*

After The Great War, the Agar Estate of tenanted properties in the village was sold off mainly to sitting tenants, so that many of the old village properties came into private hands. At the turn of the century, as can be seen from the census returns, the population had not fluctuated much since the middle of the previous century and only dipped by ten after The Great War (1914-1918). The following decade saw an increase to 475 which held steady until the 60s when numbers nearly doubled to 859 with a further increase in the 70s to 1,954.

Population increase was due to the building of post war council housing at Stone Riggs, the Kingsmoor Road development and expansion of Sandy Lane. The virtually unique linear development of the village of nearly one mile between the village name signs was maintained. In-fill and back developments albeit within the village's narrow envelope have become an ever increasing feature. Luckily a radical plan to expand the village to nearly double its size in the 1990s met with strong local opposition and had to be abandoned by the developers.

*Reference - The Victoria History of the Counties of England, Ed. Wm Page FSA 1914*

# Chapter 2

# The Shape of Things To Come

The movement towards Parliamentary Enclosure of open fields swept through England during the 18th and early 19th centuries. Most affected was a broad band from Dorset, through the Midlands and east Yorkshire to north east England. The bulk of the enclosure was between 1730 and 1830. Within this belt the prevailing system of agriculture had been an open field system with anything between two (in the earlier years) and eight or ten large fields divided into long, narrow strips (selion strips). These were allocated to members of the community but not all were eligible. In addition, there was common land for grazing, woodland for grazing swine (pannage) and various amounts of already enclosed land. It was a subsistence system and yielded limited profits. With the rising population of the time (Stockton in 1801: 225 and 1821: 450) it proved inadequate to meet local needs. Besides the rising population, another reason for the change lay in the developments in agricultural technology and methods during this period. The invention of the seed drill (by Jethro Tull), experiments in crop rotation (especially the use of turnips) and others led to the transformation of many estates into more modern producers. A prime example was the work of Thomas Coke at Holkam in Norfolk and later of Sir Thomas Sykes at Sledmere.

## Nature of the Landscape

The parish has an area of 3,200 acres. Most of the land lies between 15 and 20 metres above sea level with the highest land to the north and east of the parish. Such slight variations in micro-relief can be of major significance with regard to drainage. The whole area is part of the broad Vale of York where the underlying solid geology rarely appears on the surface. It is a product of the Pleistocene glaciation when vast ice sheets filled the Vale 10,000 years ago. These ice sheets retreated in a series of stages as temperatures rose and the subsequent melt waters left Stockton with two main kinds of deposits. On the one hand there were the fluvio-glacial sands and gravels left by streams emerging from the base of the ice. On the other, where waters stagnated into lakes, there were heavier lacustrine clays. Subsequent modifications have left a complex pattern but broadly speaking, the clays lie to the west and south of the village and the sands to the east and north. Generally, the line of the old village street marks the boundary between the two.

## The Process of Enclosure

After the application was approved by Act of Parliament (at a cost of £300), two commissioners were appointed: John Tuke of York and John Humphries of Ripon. They were paid three guineas a day and were given extensive powers. These powers included the enclosure of common lands (in the north of the parish), the over-riding of turbary rights (i.e. peat digging), the introduction of grazing rights and the creation of new roads. The commissioners also oversaw improvements made to drainage, the establishing of sand and gravel pits (there were two in Stockton) and the gating of roads to control entry into the parish. William Hotham's base map was used as reference and, in the event of a dispute, an umpire was appointed to adjudicate.

## Landholding

From a parish of 3,200 acres, only 1,200 came within the province of the enclosure commissioners. Of the rest, approximately 400 acres consisted of woodland with 1,000 acres of permanent pasture. Both these areas appear on the Hotham map as 'ancient enclosures'.

In medieval times, York was the second city of England in terms of size and population. It was hemmed in by a series of townships leaving little land available for agriculture within or in close proximity to the city boundaries. As a result, the city was forced to build up an extensive series of pasture rights over the open fields and some waste ground of the surrounding townships. By 1250 the city was gradually expanding to the north within the Forest of Galtres. Pasturage on Stockton Moor was probably enjoyed until its enclosure under the 1817 Act and Sandburn Cross is believed to mark the boundary of the York rights in this area. It may have been erected by the pasture masters in 1677 and was certainly repaired by them in 1782.

*Extract from Enclosure Map - 1817*

# Schedule C. *mentioned and referred to in and by the Award hereunto annexed.*

## West Side *of the Township of Stockton in the county of York beginning at the south end thereof.*

| Names of Owners and Proprietors of allotments in the Town's Street. | Numbers on the Plan annexed. | Lengths in Links. | Sums of which is a fine |
|---|---|---|---|
| Hall Plumer Esquire (late Wilkinson's) | 1. | 160. | 0 |
| James Kilvington Lamb Esquire as Trustee for William Richardson Esquire and Matthew Bottrill and wife | II. | 76. | 0 |
| William Richardson Esquire and Matthew Bottrill and wife | III. | 86. | 0 |
| Elizabeth Ware (widow) late Shepherd's | IV. | 40. | 0 |
| Elizabeth Ware (widow) late Slater's | V. | 60. | 0 |
| Elizabeth Ware (widow) | VI. | 58. | 0 |
| Elizabeth and Jane Ware spinsters | VII. | 257. | 0 |
| Elizabeth Ware widow | VIII. | 197. | 0 |
| William Scruton | IX. | 80. | 0 |
| Thomas Ward | X. | 70. | 0 |
| John Leak | XI. | 110. | 0 |
| William Lyth | XII. | 92. | 0 |
| George Ellin Esquire late Heselwood's | XIII. | 100. | 0 |
| Richard Selby | XIV. | 68. | 0 |
| William Wilkinson | XV. | 88. | 0 |
| Elizabeth Ware (widow) | XVI. | 322. | 0 |
| Thomas Wilkinson | XVII. | 86 | 0 |
| John Green | XVIII. | 56. | 0 |
| Benjamin Agar Esquire | XIX. | 100. | 0 |
| James Kilvington Lamb Esquire as Trustee as aforesaid | XX. | 110. | 0 |

### East Side *of the Township of Stockton aforesaid beginning at the north end there.*

| | | | |
|---|---|---|---|
| Benjamin Agar Esquire | XXI. | 104. | 0 |
| Thomas Jelson | XXII. | 143. | 0 |
| Elizabeth and Jane Ware (spinsters) | XXIII. | 82. | 0 |

*List of Land Holdings - 1817*

The pattern of allocating lands under the Enclosure Act showed considerable complexity. Some lands were held by the church and Rev William Noddins (curate of the parish which came within the control of Rev Thomas Bartholomew Woodman, prebend of Bugthorpe) who received a substantial allocation of about 100 acres. Tithes were due on this land in order to pay clergy stipends.

By far the largest landowner was Benjamin Agar with 300 acres in several parcels, some of which were also liable for tithes payable to the church. In addition some of this land was copyhold: it was covenanted for a fixed term to others. In total Benjamin Agar held 11 plots varying in size from 2 to 80 acres, although the map does not give the area of his plots in the west of the parish or the large section of the King's Moor near to the Hermitage. Of the lay landholders, the Ware family (Elizabeth and Jane) held eight plots totalling 147 acres. Other landholders with smaller allocations were Wilkinson, John Ward, Pearson, Leek, Green, Lythe, Letby, Ellen and Jebson. Some of the smaller allocations may have been compensation for the loss of common land or turbary rights. Two sand pits were established within the parish, presumably used to improve and lighten heavy clay areas. The largest of these was at Snowball (two acres) and the other was in the vicinity of Towthorpe.

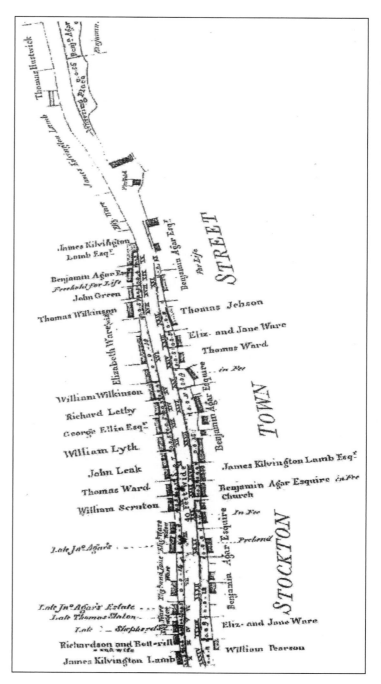

*Map of houses and occupants - 1817*

## 1817

The process of enclosure in England went on apace between 1730 and 1830. By 1820 only six counties had more than 3% as open fields. A general Enclosure Act was passed in 1801 and revised in 1845. The enclosure of Stockton (1817) was very late in the process of change to land ownership. Most areas in the Vale of York would have been enclosed before this and indeed the adjacent Vale of Pickering was complete by 1769. It is interesting to speculate about the main reason for delay but it is likely that a major obstacle was the interest of so many different parties (as listed above). Agreement would have been difficult although gradually people witnessed the benefits of new, more productive agricultural methods. Only when they understood the necessity of providing for a rapidly increasing population did the wheels of change move forward.

## A time of change

Although only approximately one third of the parish land came within the provenance of the appointed commissioners, the process brought about profound changes in the landscape. Some of the enclosures were merely an extension of previously held plots (e.g. in the case of Agar, Wilkinson, Jane and Elizabeth Ware, Hall Plummer and Ireland). The smaller enclosures may well have been given to individuals as compensation for the loss of common land and turbary rights, or the loss of a few old strips in the open fields. Among the many landscape changes it must be noted that the process did not offer fully consolidated units. The newly enclosed fields allotted to individual owners were often widely scattered. Only in the last two centuries have we seen the consolidation of farm units although the process is still not complete.

Another major change occurred with the disappearance of common lands; titles such as King's Moor and Stockton Common are now only names on the map. The pattern of settlement was profoundly affected. The map shows that almost all houses within the parish were situated along the linear village street between Stockton Hall and the site of the old Pinfold at Carr Bank Lane. Nearly all the names on the enclosure map also appear on the map of houses in the village. It was only with the increase in wealth that people could afford to move out of the village and build farmhouses situated on allocated land.

## Conclusion

It may be said that the enclosure movement made it possible for new and more scientific methods of agriculture to be adopted which led to a considerable increase in productivity. It initiated a move away from subsistence agriculture to more commercial methods. As a result, the first twenty years of the 19th century saw an increase in population made possible by improvements to water supply, sanitation and advances in medicine. However, as with any process of reform, there were winners and losers and ultimately many of the poor forfeited their rights and received limited compensation for their previously held land.

# Chapter 3

# From Stoc Tun To Stockton

In 1086 William the Conqueror ordered the compilation of the Domesday survey, listing every settlement in most parts of the country, together with landholders and their wealth. This survey was for purposes of taxation. It is interesting to note that almost all the names in our area today are included, in some form or another, in that survey.

## Stockton on the Forest

The 'ton' or 'tun' ending (meaning homestead or farm) indicates an origin in the Anglo-Saxon period. The prefix 'stock' is open to a number of interpretations. In the first place 'stoc' as in 'stockade' refers to a defended place. In view of the low lying nature of the area and the absence of any natural barriers, this interpretation would seem to be unlikely. The term 'stoc' is also used to describe the cell of a monastery and although there is much evidence of church land in the area, there is no monastic evidence. The third possibility is the most likely explanation: a derivation from the Old English 'stock' referring to cattle and 'tun' meaning farmstead or homestead. In the 14th century the name Stockton by York was used in view of its proximity to one of the major cities in the land at that time. In the 16th century the name Stockton on the Moor came into common usage. This would seem to be a reference to a considerable area of land in the north of the parish known as the King's Moor. This term was still used on the enclosure map of 1812 and found on the map of John Speed (1610). It was also in use on the maps of John Ogilby (1648), Francis Drake (1736) and the maps of Emmanuel Bowen (1750 and 1777). The modern name of Stockton on the Forest does not appear until the early 19th century and refers to the Medieval hunting forest of Galtres.

## Names within the parish

Some names recorded within the parish are of historic origin and others are modern, although still making reference to historic people or places.

### 1 Sandy Lane:

A reference to the glacial drift deposits which form the underlying surface geology of this area. There has been a history of drifts, some of these at Hazelbush recorded as two feet deep. These sandy deposits are in contrast to the lake deposits left at the end of the Ice Age which resulted in much heavier and less well drained soils.

### 2 Kingsmoor Road:

A modern name referring to the medieval King's Moor shown on the 1817 map at the northern end of the village. This also points to a link with the name Stockton on the Moor.

### 3 Chaumont Way:

Another modern name with an historic context. At the time of the Domesday Survey (1086) three carucates of land (carucates: measured amount of land ploughed in one day) were held by the canons of York and three by a major Norman landholder, Count Alan of Richmond. In 1292 three carucates were sub-let to Gaceus de Chaumont, Mayor of York.

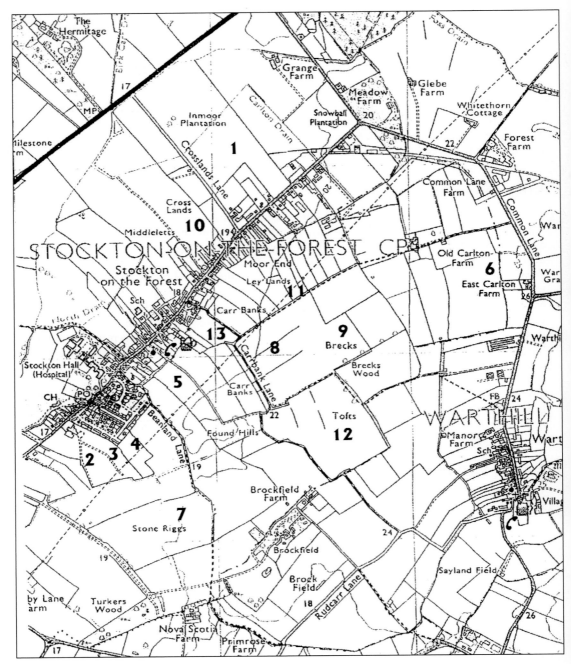

*Key to place names*

### 4 Marmian Drive:

Although referring to a medieval landowner, no specific reference has been found.


### 5 De Mauley Place:

Count Alan also sub-let three carucates of land to Peter de Mauley in 1291. This is a modern name with an historic reference.

### 6 Carleton:

The origin of this name is pre-Domesday going back to the old Scandinavian 'Karletun' which means the 'tun' or farmstead of the freemen or peasants.

### 7 Stone Riggs:

Rigg is Middle English denoting a ridge or bank. This area was enclosed well before the Enclosure Act of 1817 but the name could be a reference to the banks of open fields found in the earlier farming system.

### 8 Carr Bank Lane:

Noted on the six inch map of 1851, Carr was a pool, fen, wet or boggy land. There is still a pool there, albeit an artificial one.

### 9 Brecks (as in Brecks Wood):

Also appearing on the 6 inch map of 1851, this is the Old English term for a meadow.

### 10 Barr Lane:

Probably a reference to one of the gates mentioned after the 1817 enclosure to prevent strangers from coming into the village.

### 11 Ley Lands:

Lands which under the old open field system were fallow or untilled.

### 12 Tofts:

Late Old English or Norse meaning a homestead, often with a croft of arable land.

### 13 Cleveland Gardens:

The White Swan public house stood on the site of 98 the Village and was eventually re-named Cleveland House when the pub closed. The modern name 'Cleveland' denotes three generations of White Swan landlords.

# Chapter 4

# *Who Goes There ?*

Stockton was probably settled in the Dark Ages after 500AD. In this time many of the residents would have been required to serve in the local militia known as the levy or fyrd. As such they would have been called upon to defend their own and other villages when needed, particularly from the many overseas invaders during the period up to 1066. This year was famous for two major battles, both of which were fought within five miles of the parish. The first was at Fulford on 20 September where King Harold Hardrada of Norway and his English ally Tostig Godwinson the English king's banished brother, defeated the Northern Earls, Edwin of Mercia and Morcar of Northumberland. The second battle was at Stamford Bridge on 25 September when King Harold's and Godwinson's army defeated the previously victorious Norsemen.

In 1069 many in the North rebelled against the new Norman King William. It didn't matter to William whether the villagers of Stockton supported the rebellion or not. His troops devastated the whole of the north of England, burning villages and killing the inhabitants. When the Domesday Book was written in 1085 the parish had not recovered from this 'harrying of the north' and the land was recorded mainly as waste.

By 24 August 1453 there was 'a greate discord betwixt' the Percys and the Nevilles and the first battle in 'the beginnings of great sorrows in England' was to become known as the War of the Roses. Henry Percy, Earl of Northumberland and Richard Neville, Earl of Salisbury had been bitter rivals for a long time and things had worsened since 1452 as they tried to gain power and influence in each other's traditional territories. The fact that they both held various plots of land in the Vale of York did not help matters. In August 1453 Sir Thomas Neville married Maud Stanhope, the niece and heiress of Ralph, Lord Cromwell. The couple returned to the Neville castle at Sheriff Hutton with the groom's parents, the Earl and Countess of Salisbury.

Following the Northumberland rebellion in 1403 against Henry IV, Lord Cromwell had confiscated a number of Percy properties and the thought of these now being owned by the Nevilles did nothing to help the rivalry. Thomas Percy, Lord Egremont (the second son of Henry Percy) and his brother Richard Percy gathered a band of 1,000 retainers and arranged an ambush at Heworth Moor. Fortunately the Nevilles travelled with an escort of retainers and gave a good account of themselves. While there were altercations and threats and a fair amount of rough play, they repelled the attackers and reached home without bloodshed or any fatalities on either side.

The confrontation is currently believed to have taken place on Heworth Moor, the lower part of Monk Stray, which then extended right up to Stockton Common and Sandburn. As Sheriff Hutton is due north of Stockton, it is easy to imagine the Nevilles being forewarned of possible trouble at York with the Percys or simply by coming across 1,000 armed men waiting at Heworth Moor and that they might have veered on to the Stray to avoid an argument. They had only to venture a little over a mile to Hopgrove for this encounter to have taken place in our parish.

In 1637 Charles I had a disagreement with the Scots when he tried to impose the new Book of Common Prayer, which he was also trying to impose on the English. The Scots rebelled and Charles set about mobilising his army. In June 1639 the First Bishop's War ended with the signing of the Treaty of Berwick. In August 1640 Charles came to York as the Scots army progressed down the country, capturing Newcastle on the way. The Northern trained bands met just north of York City on the Bishop's fields around Leeman Road and on Clifton fields with a bridge of boats between them. Other troops were camped at Topcliffe, Thormanby and Tollerton. Whether they went as far out as Stockton is not recorded but they did upset one of our residents. John Agar petitioned because of the damage done to the grass on his land at Huntington by artillery horses. In October the Scots were met at Ripon where they signed the Treaty of Ripon bringing to an end the so-called Second Bishop's War.

At the start of 1644, York was King Charles's Royalist capital in the North. The Parliamentary forces lay siege to the city on 22 April that year settling around the city in a great arc. Besides a bungled breaching of St Mary's Tower and an unsuccessful attempt to destroy Walmgate Bar, the siege had little affect and, with the arrival of Prince Rupert's Royalist forces at Poppleton catching them off guard, the Parliamentarians withdrew to Marston Moor. Prince Rupert's forces spent the night in the Forest of Galtres before marching to an eventual defeat on 2 July. Two weeks later York surrendered.

In 1648 John Agar of Stockton was accused of being a delinquent Royalist. Whatever the truth, it would have been difficult for him to support Parliament publicly whilst living so close to York. If suspicions had been aroused by 1644, life in the village could have been difficult with Fairfax's troops patrolling the area.

On 13 January 1792 it is recorded that several persons of credit and respectability observed a strange atmospheric phenomenon over the woodlands on the outskirts of Stockton. This resembled a large aerial army consisting of a number of separate divisions, one of which formed a line about a mile in length. Some divisions were dressed in white uniforms and others were in black. There appeared to be a number of fir trees in the midst of the lines. These aerial troops marched in different directions, sometimes at amazing speeds with the fir trees moving with them. There were at least three other sightings of aerial armies in England between 1743 and 1820.

During the First World War it was apparent that the Government needed timber. The Forest of Galtres was an obvious source and the War Office Timber Supplies Department had a timber yard and saw mill in the field between the Station, Snowball Plantation and the end of Sandy Lane. This period also saw the beginning of Zeppelin air raids. The official advice given to York residents was to stay indoors. A number of Stockton residents are known to have disregarded this advice and risen in the early hours to watch a German Zeppelin floating majestically over Warthill on its way to bomb York. Due to its location and direction of travel it would seem that this was an L13 Zeppelin.

During the Second World War village life was noticeably affected. The close proximity of airfields like East Moor between Strensall and Sutton on the Forest meant that aircraft were a common sight. British bombers would circle overhead to gain height and then form up with those from other airfields before heading towards Hull. The noise was such that even the ground vibrated. Early on summer mornings the villagers watched for their return and wondered how some of these aircraft with silent engines and gaping holes ever managed to fly, let alone return home. German aircraft were occasionally spotted, but while there were a number of dogfights witnessed over the village, there are no official records of German plane losses in the surrounding area.

The villagers formed a Home Guard Unit as well as introducing Air Raid Precautions (ARP), Fire Wardens and a Land Army hostel. It was the job of the Home Guard, which had started as the Local Defence Force, to defend the village if the Germans invaded. They met every week for training, compulsory lectures and route marches. They had a 'dug-out' next to the road at the end of the goods sidings to use if they had to defend Warthill Station. There was also an improvised rifle range in a field near Carr Goit Bridge on the Holtby road for weapons practice. Members included Henry Elsworth (the Station Master), First World War veterans like Harry Hudson and Mr Flintoft (who used to wear his old regimental uniform) and the farmers with their workers including Robert Wright from Warthill. Henry was the leader of the Unit but Major Teulon of Hazelbush also had an involvement with the Home Guard. His connections with the local hunt enabled him to form a 'mounted squadron'. Sidney Swann, the blacksmith, became the ARP Warden for the village and Mr Smith, a

farmer from Hopgrove, also patrolled that area. There is no record of an air raid siren in the village so giving warning of bombing raids would have been part of their duties for which a whistle was issued. They also patrolled to check on blackouts, warning folk if light was visible through a window and, after a raid, confirming that all was well.

*Stockton on the Forest Home Guard - circa. 1943*

Joe Pulleyn was head of the Auxiliary Fire Service in the area and he and the other wardens had their base at Warden Jack Cusworth's home next door to Church Farm. Their job was to patrol the area and ensure that fires were extinguished properly so as not to attract the attention of enemy bombers overhead. This meant tackling any incendiary bombs which might have been dropped, by dumping them in sand or water. They also used stirrup pumps on small fires to save calling out the main Fire Service, freeing them to deal with the larger incidents.

Part of Stockton House was used as a hostel for the local group of the Women's Land Army who provided help to the local farms during the war years. This house was also the venue for a number of lantern slide shows which were put on to entertain the community during these dark times. The corrugated iron building which housed the village institute, now the scout hut, was dedicated as a first aid post during the war. Fred Sellars painted a large red cross on the roof in a 4 ft diameter white circle and the outside was stacked up with sandbags to provide protection in case of bombings. It is believed that the village school was designated as a 'rest centre' which was equipped to receive bombed-out refugees after air raids and provide them with food and shelter. There were no shelters in the village but, in case of an air raid, school children practised going to Stockton Hall and sheltering in the cellars underneath which would have given them some protection. The Hopgrove public house cellars were also available as a possible shelter. A butterfly bomb, either de-activated or a model, was taken to the school to show the children what it looked like and to alert them to its dangers.

There were a number of military camps in the area so the villagers saw lots of soldiers and military vehicles including an occasional tank. There were galvanised huts in the country lanes which stored ammunition and a searchlight battery was situated near the vicarage at Warthill. This beamed into the sky when enemy aircraft were approaching. There may also have been anti-aircraft guns nearby. At different times during the war there were three military camps in the village. The most permanent one consisted of 20 Nissen huts in the 'pony field' on the York side of Stockton Hall, now the grounds of Aspen House. York Council may have erected them to house a number of Polish refugees whilst the Army might have used them for Belgian soldiers or for men in the Searchlight Battery. The huts could also have made up a second Land Army camp. On one occasion the soldiers at the camp next to Stockton Hall threw a party for the local children and they were given rides around the field in jeeps. After the war, these huts were taken over by Flaxton Council and used for housing until the Stone Riggs estate was built.

The First World War timber yard was now just a field and a group of American servicemen pitched their tents there. The latrines must have been too basic as the men upset the railway porters by using toilet facilities at the station. The third camp was halfway down the village and was accessed via the entrance to the cricket pitch opposite the village pond. It stretched across the fields right down to Barr Lane. The closest enemy forces came to the village was as prisoners of war. Eden Camp near Malton was then a PoW camp and each day they would be taken to various farms around the area to work.

The station was busy during this war period. Normal service had been reduced to six trains a day but there were additional goods and military trains between York and Hull. These included supplies for the Russian front which were shipped from Hull and also munitions for the airfields around Pocklington and Beverley. The village witnessed a 'friendly' invasion in the form of 57 child evacuees mainly from Hull, Middlesborough and London who were housed with families in the parish. Initially this caused a problem for the primary school but after a few months places were found at other schools in the area.

On the night of Wednesday 29 April 1942 the only confirmed military action took place within the parish boundary. This was the night York was bombed. The bombers had followed the river up to York but some of the JU88s of Luftwaffe Luftlotte 3 returned home following the railway line. Whether it was a deliberate attempt to bomb Warthill station or just a desire to ditch their deadly cargo is not known. They bombed a large area of the parish from Barr Lane to Hazelbush Woods with anti-personnel butterfly bombs in a retaining canister which could hold up to 108 such bombs. One of the retaining canisters whistled over Carlton Farm and was found nearby. These deadly bombs could be triggered in a number of ways and had to be destroyed where they fell. The road from Barr Lane to the station was closed for six months and after the attack the fields were out of bounds while bomb disposal teams cleared the area. Occasional bombs were still found up until the 1950s. The only known casualty was the rector, Jack Cobham and his family, who were evacuated from the Rectory to the relative safety of Hazelbush House.

Over the centuries many men from Stockton have done military service for their Lord, King or Country. The first recorded name was Edward Hewison who served as a private soldier in the Earl of Northumberland's Light Horse and who was stationed at Sheriff Hutton castle. In 1379 the City of York had a new gallows built by Joe Penny of Blake Street at a cost of £10 15s 0d sited at York Tyburn on the Knavesmire. On 31 March 1379 Edward had the dubious honour of being the first person to be hanged at Tyburn for the rape of Louisa Bentley, a servant at the castle.

In 1920 a simple cross was erected at the entrance to Holy Trinity Church to the memory of 12 men from the parish who lost their lives during the Great War. The cross consists of an 8ft high shaft standing on octagonal steps and made of Portland stone.

*The War Memorial, Holy Trinity Church*

The 12 names recorded are:

**Major John Baillie Barstow**
Royal Engineers

**Captain Geoffrey Percy Robert Toynbee**
The Rifle Regiment, 1st Battalion Prince
Consorts Own

**Private Frank Goodall**
No. G/52238, 23rd Battalion The Duke of
Cambridge Own, The Middlesex Regiment

**2nd Lieutenant Edward Richard Scott**
No. 5343, 1st Battalion, East Yorks Regiment

**Sergeant Robert Stanley Temple**
No. 13/541, C Coy, 13th Battalion,
East Yorks Regiment

**Private Samuel Frederick Snowball**
No. 32678, 7th Battalion, Alexandra Princess
of Wales Own, The Yorkshire Regiment
(The Green Howards)

**Driver Louis R. Snowball**
No. CHT/1052, Base HT Depot (Salonika)
Army Service Corps

**Driver William Marshall**
No. T4/211023, HT Unit Army Service
attached to 231 Field Ambulance, Royal
Army Medical Corps

**Private Walter Sellers**
No.47111, (10th Service Battalion) 50th
Brigade, 17th Divn.VI Corps. The Prince of
Wales Own, The West Yorks Regiment

**Sergeant J W Smith**
Royal Warwickshire Regiment

**Private D Harrison**
Grenadier Guards

**Private F Collinson**
The Middlesex Regiment

*Two other volunteers with connections to the village are known to have died in the conflict:*

**Private Alexander Hetherton**
No. 2213, East Riding Yeomanry (son of John Hetherton of Sandburn)

**Private Harold Jeremiah Bratley**
No. 22717, Y Coy, 18th Battalion Lancashire Fusiliers (born in Stockton on the Forest on 25
December 1886 and moved to Gate Helmsley with his parents before the war started)

*In 2002 the memorial was cleaned and an inscription to one of Stockton's fallen was added:*

**Flight Sergeant David Hartnell Wright (Air Gunner)**
No.1622986, 311 Ferry Training Flight, Royal Air Force Volunteer Reserve

*Holy Trinity Churchyard is recognised as a site of war graves by the Commonwealth War Graves Commission. There are five servicemen from WWII remembered on gravestones in the cemetery but only David Wright is named on the village's war memorial. The others are:*

**Captain Basil Fleury-Teulon**
No.95210, 5th Royal Inniskilling Dragoon Guards, Royal Army Corps.

**Petty Officer Henry Todd (Stoker)**
No. P/K1632, Royal Navy, HMS Victory
**Sergeant Harold Robert Thompson (Navigator)**
No.R/166511 Royal Canadian Air Force

**Leading Seaman  Robert Thompson**
No.C/JX 185536, HMS President III  Royal Navy (Robert was Harold's English cousin from Middlesex. He was lost at sea in the Atlantic near the Canadian coast and his name has been added to Harold's gravestone as a memorial.)

Military life still has an influence on the village today. For the past 120 years there has been constant military activity just over the parish border. The Army established a camp before 1890, later to become a permanent training camp and rifle range at Strensall. Over the years the wind has carried the sound of various small arms fire from the Martini Henry to the rapid automatic fire of the L85A2 rifle.

# Chapter 5

# Stockton Rifles

At the turn of the 19th century, Britain and France were still engaged in their centuries long on/off warfare. While its regular army was for service overseas, Britain's main defence at home was the Militia. A yearly ballot was held of all able-bodied men who were compelled to serve for four years. Many hated the system and it was not unknown, particularly in the farming communities, for fathers to break the trigger finger of their sons in the hope that a deformed finger would make it impossible for them to serve. In 1803 with invasion imminent, King George III instigated new laws to create a part-time volunteer force. These men trained and stayed in their home district, allowing them to continue with their usual occupations for most of the year.

*Captain Ware*
*reproduced by kind permission of Will Garton-Jones*

The meeting for Stockton's district, Bulmer, was held at The White Horse in St Marygate, York on 15 August 1803. It was attended by Benjamin Agar of Brockfield Hall in his role as a Deputy Lieutenant of the County. The Deputy Lieutenants were responsible for organising this volunteer force. It is assumed that, as they were neighbours and also related, Benjamin discussed this with Rev John Ware of Stockton Hall. As a result on 28 August 1803 Rev Ware's offer to raise the Stockton Forest Volunteer Corps of Riflemen was graciously accepted by his Majesty.

The Rifle Corps was dressed in a rifle green uniform with black lace collars and cuffs and armed with an early version of the British Infantry rifle (which was developed in 1800 and now commonly named after its designer Ezekiel Baker). Besides a contribution of £30 from John Agar of Warthill and a clothing allowance of £1 per man which could be claimed every three years, Rev Ware paid all the costs to clothe and arm the Corps. The men were expected to train for 20 days a year, to have regular inspections and to attend training camps as necessary. They were paid the full army rate of 1s 0d a day for privates and bugler, 1s 2d for corporals and 1s 6d for sergeants. 9s 5d was paid to Rev Ware as captain and his brother William Ware received 5s 8d as lieutenant. From 1806 the officers were not paid and corporals and sergeants only received 1s 0d per day. Sergeant John Wilkinson must have done some previous military service as he was made permanent drill sergeant on 29 April 1805 for which he received a daily allowance of 6d (for 365 days a year) in lieu of pay. The Rifle Unit had buglers rather than the drummers in the regular Infantry. A bugler didn't appear on the pay lists until April 1804, a few months after a 'wanted' advert had been placed in a York newspaper:

*'For a CORPS of RIFLEMEN,*
*A PERSON capable of Blowing the BUGLE.*
*Liberal Encouragement will be given'.*

The applicant had to apply to the printer so it can only be speculated that this was for our Rifles. However, the first bugler was not a Stockton man.

Inspections were held up to six times a year during which the Corps performed their drills, manoeuvres, skirmishes, loading and firing on the ground before an Inspecting Field Officer. He usually expressed his approbation of their good appearance, the excellence of their arms and considered them fit for any service. They attended full time training camps twice at Scarborough, once for three weeks in 1805 and again for two weeks in 1808. It was a two day march to and from the village for which they received an allowance above their pay, plus an allowance for the transport of baggage and overnight accommodation at an inn on route. These camps were meant to give volunteers experience of acting in a military fashion with other corps and regular soldiers. Regular discipline, correctness of dress and military appearance were emphasised and they also received pay, franking privileges at the post office and allowances if injured on duty. Many hours were spent exercising every morning and parading each evening. They also performed guard duty for stores and ammunition and prepared for the occasional review by the Inspecting Field Officer.

The King's birthday fell during both occasions when they were in Scarborough. A three-volley Royal Salute was fired on the beach together with the other units stationed there. In 1804 the Corps marched in honour of the King's birthday in a grand military parade from Bootham Bar to Fulford where the Royal Salute was given. The men, aged between 17 and 55, all came from Stockton and the surrounding villages. The style and variation of spellings on the pay lists show a possible 130 names and with common surnames and family forenames it is difficult to establish true identities. At least one father and son (William Lund senior & junior) served together and there were three John Pearson names. Six men from the Wilkinson family joined up: Charles, James, William, Robert (three men having the same name with connections to the village) and two Johns. With so many having the same name, identifying the drill sergeant is difficult.

Rev Ware was not the village priest but during his period of commanding the Corps he did occasionally carry out ministerial duties at Holy Trinity Church. He conducted the marriage ceremonies for two of his men. Rifleman John Potter married Mary Pearson in 1803 and Rifleman Marmaduke Stothard married Jane Jebson in 1808. Two other riflemen were also married during this period - George Hustwick in 1805 and Thomas Hustwick in 1808. Neither was in service at the time of their weddings and Minister John Overton conducted their services.

After 1806 King George realised that the volunteer system had been too successful and there was a lack of men going into full time military units. As well as reducing some of the volunteers' pay in this year, other gradual changes were made to their conditions. This caused a decline in their numbers across the country until 1808 when the volunteers were actively encouraged to join their local militia. Some units did remain in service until 1816.

On 16 September 1808 Rev Ware died of consumption. He was buried in Holy Trinity churchyard on 22 September, presumably with full military honours and a gun salute. His brother William took over command but the services of the Corps were withdrawn soon afterwards. The men appear to have been very loyal as their numbers had remained stable, averaging around 64 men throughout the years. Perhaps the combination of changes to their conditions of service and their captain's death was sufficient for them to call it a day. A number from other local volunteer corps did join the militia but there is no evidence to suggest that any of the Rifles joined up.

## To Hull and back with Captain Ware

In 1804 the Corps took part in a secret experiment. Twenty two men rode from York to Hull on what was described as 'a machine' covering the journey there and back in ten hours, including a two hour break in Hull. An average of over ten miles per hour was maintained despite problems with the horses' harness and a wheel bearing catching fire. The 'machine' is believed to have been built by Lieutenant Colonel Crichton of the Edinburgh Volunteers whose family business involved the building of coaches and carriages. They had recently passed through York on their way to London in a similarly described 'machine' which had four wheels and was pulled by four horses on which were two postillion. In September 1804 the Duke of York officially acknowledged Colonel Crichton as the inventor of the 'machine' for the 'speedy conveyance of troops'.

# Chapter 6

# *Stockton Hall*

This impressive dwelling was built on land owned by Hall Plummer where he and his wife Harriet lived with their eight daughters and two servants. A theory exists that a hall was previously built here between 1750 and 1780 by a West Riding mine owner. He wanted a country mansion in the York area. Mr Plummer demolished this existing hall to build his new one. The present hall was probably built between 1820 and 1830. It consists of a three storey, double entry, five bay house with servants' quarters to the right of the main house. There was a fine stable block with clock tower, walled garden, extensive formal gardens and drive from Malton Road where a gate keeper's lodge was situated.

The buildings are Grade I listed and their official listing documentation is as follows:

*House circa. 1800. Brick in Flemish bond, Welsh slate roof. Central-entry double-pile plan with service wing to right. 3 storeys, 5 bays. Main façade: plinth broken by Ionic porch with paired columns containing double-leaf glazed door beneath radial fanlight. Sashes with glazing bars on continuous sill to ground and first floors, that above door in eared and shouldered architrave with pediment. Second floor: 6-pane sashes, that to centre in eared and shouldered architrave. Moulded cornice. Hipped roof with stacks rising through pitch of roof. Garden façade has similar glazing, but with central pedimented bay breaks forward slightly, with 3-window bow to ground floor and Venetian window to first floor. Interior: blind round-headed arcades to entrance hall which terminates in an arch carried on composite columns, 3 blind arches to spinal corridor with fluted pilaster to right.*

*Pevsner, N Yorkshire: the North Riding 1966*

*Stable block to Stockton Hall (qv). circa. 1800. Brick in Flemish bond, Welsh slate roof. 2 storeys, 9 bays. Central bay and paired outer bays break forward slightly. Central elliptical-arched double door flanked by 6-panel doors and 16-pane sashes. First floor: 8-pane sashes with alternate windows blocked. Cambered brick arches throughout. Hipped roof. Central bell turret with clock to base and bell housed beneath dome carried on fluted columns surmounted by weather vane.*

The hall was situated in a small wooded estate with the boundary wall adjacent to the main street, the alignment of which was changed in the 1960s. The tradesmen's entrance was accessed via two large iron gates with pillars opposite what is now Stone Riggs. The main entrance then was reached from the new Malton Road opposite North Lane where there was a gatekeeper's lodge and long drive through the estate. Carriages entering that way approached the rear of the hall with its large bay window passing by the York side of the property. Visitors alighted at the main entrance which faced the village.

In 1835 on the death of Harriet Plummer, the hall was sold to George John Lloyd. On his death in 1863 the hall passed to his daughter Alicia Maria Lloyd whose brother, Rev George Lloyd Graeme, inherited the Yarburgh Graeme Estate (later Yarburgh of Heslington).

Alicia Maria instigated the building of St Paul's Church, Heslington in 1857-8 at a cost of £3,500. Miss Lloyd was most generous to the village with endowments to the church and for the establishment of the school. She died in 1892 at the age of 77. It is said that, whilst not officially Lady of the Manor, she was regarded as such by everyone and was even considered as 'minor royalty'.

The hall's ownership passed to George William Lloyd of Caythorpe, Lincolnshire but was occupied by Mrs Palmes

*Aerial view - circa. 1900*

(later of the Cunard family) until 1901 when George William Lloyd, MA and JP, returned to live there until his death in 1937. His widow lived there until she died in 1947. Mr Horsley owned the hall for a short time until Mr Pedley bought the property and ran a garment factory there from about 1950 to 1960. It remained un-occupied until 1964 when York City Council acquired it for use as an Approved School. North Yorkshire County Council then took it over as a Community Home with Education. In 1989 it passed to AMI Healthcare/Partnerships in Care as a secure Psychiatric Hospital and remains so to the present day.

*Basil Metcalfe (Deputy Head), Marjorie Evans (Matron), Ned Evans (Head) - 1966*

The stable block has alternate windows to the first floor blocked up. This was to avoid Window Tax which, although established in the reign of William III, was amended in 1825 to include houses and buildings with more than seven windows.

The 'Pink Lady' is said to haunt the main building although she is not mentioned in any documents relating to the hall's history.

# Chapter 7

# The Village & Monuments

## Brockfield Lodge

This impressive property was built in 1824 and stood on the long drive to Brockfield House, home of the Agar family, lords of the manor. However, it was demolished in 2008 due to planning rules following the construction of detached property on the site. It had a recessed walkway with 3 round pillars supporting the roof overhang. On the accommodation elevation, under the overhang, there were 3 ecclesiastic shape windows similar to those to the frontage of Stockton House. The other 3 sides to the building, single storied, were very plain and roughly rendered; a continuous cast-iron roof tie belt ran around the building. A pantile roof with two strange chimney stack arrangements – the one nearest the road had two Elizabethan style brick chimneys, while the one furthest from the road had a six sided stack, with 2 round brick chimneys.

## 69 The Village (Grade II listed)

Built mid to late 18th century of brick in Flemish bond with pantile roof. It has a first floor band, 4-pane sash windows throughout, cogged eaves course, gable coping, end stacks and tumbling-in to gable ends.

## Stockton Grange and attached outbuildings (Grade II listed)

Designed by Walter Brierley for W A Pearson, the Grange was built in 1907. Red brick in English bond under a tiled roof, the house forms an 'L' shape around the entrance forecourt. The main house has an entrance porch leading to the hallway from which drawing room, dining room and kitchen lead off. The service wing forms the 'L'. The drawing room has French windows to the rear garden and a square bay to the side. On this wing of the house the double string course is designed to give a jettied effect, while elsewhere it is more conventional. The windows are a mix of casement and sash with small panes and they vary in size and height. At the back of the house a curved course of bricks below the central window reflects the flattened arch above this and most of the other windows. Tile is used to form kneelers at the corners of the gables and the cast iron gutter supports are finished with a restrained decorative curl. The outbuilding alongside the servants' wing is also in English bond with the same use of tiles and gutter supports and with hand made external hinges on the doors. A chimney stack suggests this was the original washhouse with coal house and store behind. A further outbuilding, probably a later addition, is of similar design but uses stretcher bond without the distinctive hinges and gutter supports. Close by is a small outbuilding with a hipped roof built in Flemish bond brick (probably not original).

The interior retains a large number of original features, however only one of the original fireplaces (in the dining room) remains and the layout of the upper floor has been altered. The internal doors and door surrounds are original although some have been moved. All retain brass handles and lock mechanisms, those in the servants' quarters having visible lock housing while those in the main house have mechanisms hidden. The parquet floor in the hall and the plain staircase are also original. The windows retain their brass furniture and plain rolled moulding on the frame. In 1907 the house cost £1,431.

## 71 The Village *(Grade II listed)*

An early 19th century cottage built in brick in Flemish bond, French tile roof, central hallway entry, 2 storeys, 3 bays, 4-panel door beneath divided overlight. Sashes with glazing bar beneath segmental brick arches throughout. First floor band. End stacks and tumbling-in to gable ends. It is said that Mrs Rhoda Scott who lived at No. 79 witnessed a ghostly apparition passing through the passage way between Nos. 71 and 73 heading in the direction of the chapel.

## 73 The Village

An 18th century cottage owned originally by the Sowray family who farmed land where the golf course is situated - hence 'Sowray's Trod' leading to it. During the war, power cables ran down the Trod to the military establishment at the Hall. There was a water pump at the road side.

## Elm Tree Farm, 74 The Village *(Grade II listed)*

Mid-late 18th century with 20th century renovations. Brick in Flemish bond, 20th century pantile roof. Central hallway entry, 2 rooms in depth. 2 storeys, 3 bays. 20th century half-glazed door in door-case flanked by 16-pane sashes. Band. Sash windows with glazing bars flanked by 16-pane sashes. Flat brick arches throughout. Dentilled eaves course. Gable coping, end stacks. Interior: large elliptical-arched fireplace to drawing room. Attic still contains old farm winch.

## Park Farm House, 77 The Village *(Grade II listed)*

Early 18th century with 20th century alterations. Brick in random bond, 20th century concrete Roman tiles, 3-cell lobby entry plan with staircase in flat turret to rear. 2 storeys, 3 first floor windows. 20th century board door beneath cambered brick arch with unsympathetic 20th century bow windows to left and right. Double band. First floor: 16-pane sashes beneath flat brick arches to central window rendered. Evidence for blocked window above door. Dentilled eaves course. Gable coping, left end and ridge stack, with external stack to right end. Interior: contains original closed-string dog-leg staircase with squat turned balusters and a ramped handrail.

## 85 The Village

Initially built in 1908 this is a fine Edwardian style house. It was built by the Lloyd family as accommodation for their chauffeur with excellent wood finishes throughout, said to resemble those of the hall itself. It is believed that a matching property was to have been built adjacent to it on what is now the scout hut site but this was delayed and finally dropped with the outbreak of the Great War. When the site on the other side became available for development at the turn of this millennium the planners insisted that its design should mirror the original as near as possible. Thus in 2001 No. 83 was built and is one of the more 'in keeping' of the new builds in the village.

## 92 The Village *(Grade II listed)*

1781 house with cross wing of 18th century brick in Flemish bond, Roman tile roof. Central hallway entry, 2 rooms in depth with cross wing to rear. 2 storeys, 3 first floor windows. 20th century glazed door with divided overlight. Sashes with glazing bars beneath flat brick arches throughout. Gable coping, end stacks. Tumbling-in to gable ends. Interior: fine open-string staircase with 2 turned square-knob balusters to each step. Believed initially to have been Ham Farm, evidence that Tom Wilkinson paid land tax in 1781 and the initials TW can still be seen in metal ties in each gable end. However the Enclosures map of 1815 shows the property in the hands of Thos. Ward so they might be his initials. Known to have had two very fine Adams fireplaces ripped out in the 70s, it is believed in the march for modernisation! This building was the Post Office for many years until its closure in 2000. In the 1800s the post was delivered from and despatched to York by foot arriving at 8am leaving at 4.30pm; this became inward at 6.50am & 4.30pm and outward 6.55am & 5pm with the introduction of cycle post in early 1900. Whilst we now have a door step delivery once a day, sadly we have regressed to only one collection per day!

## 93 The Village *(Grade II listed)*

Early 19th century house. Brick with Flemish bond, French tiled roof. Hallway entry with service wing of separate build to left. 2 storeys, symmetrical 3-bay façade with main house defined by quoins in orange brick and single-bay service wing. 20th century glazed door with overlight flanked by 4-pane sashes beneath brick relieving arches. Service wing has 4-pane sashes beneath cambered arch. Band to main house only. First floor: 4-pane sashes all beneath segmental brick arches. Dentilled eaves course. Gable coping, end and ridge stacks. Tumbling-in to gable ends. For some time the service wing to left was used as a village shop.

## Orchard Garth, 98 The Village
### (Formerly White Swan Inn and Cleveland House)

Records show a house was built in 1735 and given to Elizabeth Kershaw by her father, a glove maker in the city of York, along with many acres of land on her marriage to Seth Agar. Tadcaster Tower Brewery turned it into a public house in 1835. In its later years three sisters tenanted it with their brother called Cleveland. Trade gradually declined and the licence was finally given up in 1947. Originally a butcher's shop was attached to the public house. The property was thought to house three or four workers cottages - to a ground floor of 2" bricks with the first floor being added when it became a public house built with 2.5" bricks. This avoided the new brick tax as larger bricks meant fewer were used. Probably thatched originally – heightened gable ends being used to hold thatch in place at ends of property. A low ground floor extension formed the cellar area from which beer in jugs was served straight from the wooden barrels through a two way cupboard servery to the front parlour. The doors opened flat to walls avoiding beer spillage by people behind them and allowing visiting constabulary to be seen immediately on entry!

## Stockton House, 105 The Village *(Grade 11 listed)*

House built circa. 1800. Brick in English bond with stucco front, Welsh slate roof. Hallway entry. 2 storeys, 6 bays. 6-fielded-panel door beneath radial fanlight in door-case with cornice carried by brackets to fourth bay. 2 sashes with glazing bars to left, with first bay blind. 2 pointed sashes with glazing bars with Gothic glazing, hood-moulds and label-stops to tight. Band. First floor: sashes with glazing bars to left, pointed windows as ground floor but lacking hood-moulds and label-stops to right. Plain coped parapet conceals hipped roof. The first Methodist chapel in the village was incorporated into this house. Miss Kershaw lived here for many years and it is reported that she looked out from an upper floor window most of the day and the young girls of the village would curtsey to her as they passed. During the Second World War it was the home for Land Army girls working in the area. Chicory growing sheds in garden to rear from about this time still remain.

## Forest House, 107 The Village *(Grade 11 listed)*

Early 19th century house. Brick in Flemish bond, pantile roof. Central hallway entry plan, 2 storeys, 3 first floor windows, 4-panel door with overlight in door-case. Casements beneath cambered brick arches throughout. Gable coping, end stacks. Tumbling-in to gable ends.

## Holly Tree House, 108 The Village

Property is first described in an Abstract of Title dd 1870 (but is obviously earlier) as being owned by Miss Harriet Elizabeth Agar of Brockfield Hall who died in 1904; the Agar family having been Lords of the Manor since circa. 1580. Her Estate was administered by Trustees – Charles Talbot Agar of Brockfield Hall, Cecil Hilton Hutton Wybergh of Overton Hall Ellesmere and Alexander Forbes of Stamford Bridge House. As with much of the Estate which owned many of the properties in Stockton on the Forest, the property was conveyed/sold in 1921 to purchasers who were sitting tenants or with the sitting tenants retaining leases. Formerly know as Holly Tree Farm. The village mill was situated on the slight rise to the rear.

## Providence Farmhouse

Victorian built farmhouse in a similar style to the majority of village properties, with interesting features. Previously called Providence House, it was a dairy farm in the early 1900s. Land to rear has evidence of 'ridge and furrow' cultivation.

*Deeds of land for Providence Farmhouse dating from 1809*

## Hollyroyd, Sandy Lane

By Indenture dated 10/07/1921 – Vendors Charles Talbot Agar [i], Cecil Hilton Wybergh & Alexander Forbes [ii] Trustees of the Estate of Harriet Elizabeth Agar deceased *[06/07/1901 – bequeathed all property to William Talbot Agar then to son Charles Talbot Agar]* to purchaser [iii] William Brown for £275. Property being specified as 2 roods 14 perches part of field 154 now in occupation of purchaser/tenant. The house was renamed Hollyroyd in 1921 - believed initially to have been two shepherds cottages, the original being built of 2.5" clamp bricks used in Georgian period, upper floor being 3" (brick tax introduced in 1784 being reason for size change). The pattern is believed to be 'garden wall bond' post 1720.

## The Old Rectory, Sandy Lane *(Grade II listed)*

Purpose built Victorian rectory. Built in 1865 in polychrome brick with a Welsh slate roof incorporating bands of fish-scale slates. Parallel spinal ranges with pair of gabled cross wings to front. Main façade: 2 storeys, 2 first floor windows. Gabled porch on carved capitals contains half-glazed door with fanlight. To left: a pair of plate glass sashes beneath parapet with polychrome diaper motif, continuous with first floor band. To right: 3 small pointed windows beneath rubbed brick arches, all beneath low roof, hipped to right. First floor: left gable, slightly larger than that to right, contains pair of plate glass sashes beneath stone lintel and brick relieving arch. To right: a pair of trefoil-headed windows. Gable coping. Eaves stack to left. Ridge stack to spinal-range.

# The Monuments

## The War Memorial

Erected in 1920 after the Great War of 1914-18 in Portland stone. The memorial is 8 ft tall and surmounted by a cross with halo. It stands on a two tier octagonal plinth beside the gate to Holy Trinity church. The original cost was £120. Initially placed to record the names of those who died in that conflict. The dead of 1939-45 are also remembered.

## Sandburn Cross

In grounds of Sandburn House, approx 100m north of Tanglewood Inn - boundary marker 1677 *(see right)*. Inscription possibly one from an earlier cross shaft. Made of limestone, it has a square section base approx. one metre square and 0.25 metres in height. There are inscriptions to each face. To south: *Ebor Monkstray. Mat. Walls. Jo Blackburn. John Beforth. Edgeforth. Pasture Masters 1677.* To east: *This cross repaired in the year 1782 by Wm. Bamburgh, John Dale, Jos. Gorwood, Ric'd. Pearson - Pasteur Masters.* To west: *This Cross was blown down by the great wind on the 7th of January 1839 and repaired by her Grace the Duchess of Sutherland 1840.* To north: *Restored by John Hetherton in 1912.*

The ashes of John Hetherton, who died 14 February 1937 aged 74, lie around this stone. Folklore has it that Old Mother Shipton prophesied that the world would end if the cross should fall down three times! As she 'lived' 200 years before the cross was even erected, this would appear to be a myth. The stone is currently in a poor state and the History Group is itself attempting to make repairs.

## Milepost

Late 19th century - south of Stockton Hermitage *(see left)*. Made by Mattisons of Bedale. Cast iron. Triangular section with sloping upper face. Inscription: Left face: *Malton 13 miles* below pointing hand. Right face: *York 5 miles* below pointing hand. Reverse: manufacturer's name. This post had been stolen and was offered for sale on eBay! Fortunately, it was recovered by the police and replaced courtesy of The Milestone Society in 2008.

## Milepost

Late 19th century - south of Hazlebush Café. Made by Mattisons of Bedale. Cast iron. Triangular section with sloping upper face. Inscription: Left face: *Malton 12 miles* below pointing hand. Right face: *York 6 miles* below pointing hand. Reverse: manufacturer's name.

*The milestones on Malton Road are also Listed Monuments.*

# Chapter 8

# *Holy Trinity Church*

*Stockton on the Forest Church prior to its restoration*

The present church dates from the re-building carried out in 1895. The first recorded chapel here was in 1276 when, granting the tithes of the land in Carlton and Sandburn to the chapel of Stockton, the Archbishop of York said that this land had been newly brought back to arable status and so had become subject to tithing. Whether Stockton had a chapel previously is not known, as the entry in the Domesday Book (1086) records that, in common with much of the north of England, Stockton had been laid waste six years earlier by William the Conqueror as reprisal for the rebellion against him. At that time it was estimated that Stockton consisted of six carucates of land (about 1,000 acres) one half of which was owned by the canons of York Minster who also claimed three carucates each from Carlton and Sandburn. The other half was owned by Count Alan of Richmond.

The name 'Stockton Chapel' indicates that it was connected to another church at Bugthorpe. The administration of York Minster was being reformed by Archbishop Thomas who created a large number of canons to run the Minster. These canons were made rectors of village churches whose prebend (salary) was often augmented by other churches. Thus the Canon of Bugthorpe received the financial benefits of the chapel in Stockton: *a mill and tithes in Stockton, the farm of Marton and a manor house in the city of York*, which in 1291 had a value of £40. In return for these benefits he had to provide a church building and an assistant priest for services there, a situation which continued until 1840.

The amount spent on Stockton by the canon of Bugthorpe was meagre. In his visitation of 1615 Archbishop Toby Matthews found Stockton Chapel in a ruinous state; the roof lacking tiles and the windows broken. In 1743 Archbishop Herring found that services were only held once a fortnight and were taken by the Rector of St Margaret's, Walmgate. In 1738, 1788 and again in 1810 the church authorities allocated the rents of certain lands in Aughton on Derwent, Castleford and elsewhere.

Much support was given by the parishioners themselves. The chalice given in 1735 by Mary Agar, whose family had become Lords of the Manor of Stockton, is evidence of this. By 1840 the chapel was once again in a dilapidated condition and consequently, under Archbishop Vernon-Harcourt, the connection with Bugthorpe was severed. From then onwards the archbishop appointed a priest.

In 1843 at a cost of only £650, which was a small sum even for those days, the nave of the church was re-built. The whole village helped with the transport of material to make considerable savings on the building work. Benjamin Agar of Brockfield gave £100 and George Lloyd of Stockton Hall seems to have contributed the rest. The architect was G T Andrews of York. A parsonage house was provided for the first time in 1865 and two years later the Ecclesiastical Commission declared the parochial chapelry of Stockton to be a rectory.

Until the late 19th century the fortune of the church revolved round such families as the Agars of Brockfield, the Lloyds of Stockton Hall, the Rawdons of the Hermitage and the Barstows of Hazel Bush. Captain Lewis Barstow RN had married Mary Anne, elder daughter of John Agar. Although the Agars were Lords of the Manor, their home at Brockfield was some distance from the village and it was the Lloyd family of Stockton Hall, previously of Manchester, who took responsibility for village matters. Alicia Maria Lloyd was a great benefactress to the church and village. In 1856, using an older charity of Susannah Wilkinson, she provided for the free teaching of ten scholars and erected a handsome schoolhouse with a master's house attached. Village life was further enriched by the establishment in 1856 of a church institute with a reading room and lending library. In 1893 the parish room was built. The rector of Stockton, Rev William Gell, was at the centre of these activities, supported by the Agar and Lloyd families and the village community.

*Above:*
*The Agar Family Crest*

*Right:*
*The Lloyd Family Crest*

In 1878 village co-operation was illustrated by the influence of the two Agar sisters, Mrs Mary Anne Barstow and Miss Harriet Elizabeth Agar and Rev Henry Hassard. The two sisters, as joint lords of the manor, objected strongly to the rector's re-arrangement of the chancel. This positioned the Agar family pew face-to-face with those occupied by the workers of the Brockfield estate. The matter went to the archbishop's consistory court and was decided in favour of the sisters due to a petition from all of the villagers (except for one family) who supported the Agar objection.

## The Re-building of the Church in 1895

By 1890 the much repaired chancel was once again in a poor state and out of commission. As the population of the village was growing, plans were set in motion by Rev William Gell to re-build the chancel and enlarge the nave. Early ideas by Temple Moore were rejected as 'something queer' and a more orthodox plan by Naylor & Sale of Derby was accepted. The 1843 nave had been designed in early English gothic style consistent with the medieval chancel and carried out in white brick with stone facings. The new plan reflected this gothic style with the nave retained but extended one bay eastwards. The chancel was completely re-built but the west gallery, the west wall and the bell gallery were all demolished. A baptistry and a clergy vestry were added on either side of the existing porch. There were plans for transepts and an apse to the baptistry but these were abandoned. Lancet windows were inserted in the new west wall and a new bell tower with steeple was erected.

*The interior of Holy Trinity Church*

Since most of the cost was met by the Agar sisters, the arms of the Agar family are to be found on the east gable of the chancel but there were other contributors including the Lloyds of Caythorne Hall, the Palmes of Naburn, the Duke of Sutherland and the Archbishop of York. At this time several of the fitments were renewed and the major donations were

- Altar crosses, vases and candlesticks given by Miss Edith Palmes
- The pulpit with marble columns given by the family of Rev William Gell
- Brass and iron lectern given by Captain Bairstow
- Glastonbury chairs given by Rev Canon Rawdon

Linen frontals and hassocks, all carefully hand-worked, were presented by various families in the village. The Lloyd family donated an organ and four more bells in memory of Alicia Lloyd who had died in 1892. The church was re-opened with great ceremony by William MacLagan, Archbishop of York, on 6 January 1896.

## The 20th Century

The church was served by many fine priests including Rev William Gell and the biblical scholar Rev Charles Mackie. Many families in the village provided church wardens, prominent among whom were the Beales, the Snowballs, the Sterrikers, the Marshalls and the Broadleys. The church was further enriched by gifts from parishioners: Miss Hunt and Miss Yeomans contributed frontals and covers while the family of Canon Rawdon was also particularly generous. In 1919 the entrance to the churchyard was improved by the erection of a low and entrance gates with a simple dignified cross of Portland stone nearby. This commemorated the twelve Stockton men who fell in the Great War of 1914-18. In 1939 Holy Trinity became the mother church for the local parishes of Warthill and Holtby with the union of the benefices. The problem of patronage was solved in 1958 when the decision was made that it should alternate between the crown and the archbishop.

The present church owns many artifacts including one of only three pre-Reformation chalices in England, currently held in York Minster. The bell shaped bowl with baluster stem is engraved with the Agar arms (a chevron between three boars' heads couped) and is inscribed *'The gift of Mrs Margaret Agar, daughter of Thomas Agar Esq. 1735'*. The cup was made by Thomas Waite of York in 1654 and is hallmarked TW in monogram, small italic X  Leop. And lys.

A patten inscribed *'This belongs to Stockton Chapel 1736'* is possibly London 1709.

The windows are worthy of inspection:

The three-light east window was presented in 1895 by Miss Harriet Agar and her sister Mrs Bairstow (made by T F Curtis of Ward & Hughes, London)

Also in 1895, two of the three windows in the vestry south of the porch were given by the Kershaw family of Stockton House and the third given by parishioners (T F Curtis)

The stained glass windows in the south nave were presented by Miss Agar and the Pearson family of Warthill Grange Farm (T F Curtis)

The windows on the north side were later presented by the Pearson family

The fine west window was given by Francis Rawdon in 1928 in memory of her daughter Dorothea (M Powell of London)

The window in the chancel is dedicated to the memory of Dr John Ellerker, a devoted local doctor, who attended the villagers from 1970 until his sudden death in 1988.

*The Ellerker Window*

In 1923 Francis Rawdon gave the chancel screen and reredos to the church. They were both designed by E R Walker of York and crafted by The Mouseman of Kilburn, Robert Thompson. Rawdon also donated the choir stalls and altar rails to the church in 1930.

The organ, which was built in 1896 by Forster and Andrews, was given to the church by the Lloyds. In 1932 an electric blower was installed, much to the delight of those who had previously had to hand-pump the organ. The organ was renewed in 1942 and a complete overhaul was undertaken in 1951. A thorough restoration was carried out by 7internationally renowned as organ builders and fulfilled many prestigious commissions in every part of the British Isles and overseas; their instruments had a reputation for musical and mechanical excellence.

*The Mouseman's signature carving*

## The History of the Bells

The chapel probably always had at least one bell during its history. Three bell foundries existed in York in 1800. An old photograph dated circa. 1890 shows two bells hung in a gable to the west end of the nave.

In 1895 four bells were cast by John Taylor & Co. of Loughborough and were hung in cast iron H frames with plain bearings and Hastings stays. Bells 3 to 6 were given by G W Lloyd in memory of his aunt Miss Alicia M Lloyd. In the 1970s maintenance was carried out under the direction of Tower Captain, John Ducker. After 84 years the fittings were in need of a major overhaul. In 1979 stage one of the repairs was begun with work on the tower and transportation undertaken by Alan Hearn, the new Tower Captain. At a branch meeting it was decided to put two new bells in the tower. David Potter led the team of John Ducker and Alan and Pat Hearn, together with assistance from many other friends. In 1983 Michael King, the Tower Captain, organised a marathon ring on hand bells by schoolchildren.

### Description of the Bells:

| | | | |
|---|---|---|---|
| Treble | 2cwt 1qtr | 114 kg | |
| Second | 2cwt 1qtr | 114 kg | |
| Third | 2cwt 1qtr | 114 kg | 'We praise thee' |
| Fourth | 3cwt 1qtr | 165 kg | 'We bless thee' |
| Fifth | 4cwt 1qtr | 216 kg | 'We give thanks to thee' |
| Sixth | 5cwt 3qtr | 292 kg | 'O Lord God Almighty' |

# Names of priests recorded at Holy Trinity Church

| Curates/Incumbents | | Rectors | | Curate in Charge | |
|---|---|---|---|---|---|
| 1646 | J Crawford | 1710 | H Howlett | 2002 | Mary E Willetts |
| 1791 | Moore | 1885 | W Gell | | |
| 1650 | Pennell | 1716 | W Keys | **Priest in Charge** | |
| 1791 | J Ware | 1900 | J Roy | 2008 | N Bird |
| 1653 | Harwood | 1718 | T Kaley | | |
| 1792 | J Overton | 1902 | E C Mackie | | |
| 1660 | A Hare | 1721 | W Watson | | |
| 1809 | W Noddins | 1935 | C Reed | | |
| 1680 | T Kettlewell | 1722 | T Kaley | | |
| - | J Jones | 1939 | J H A Cobham | | |
| 1685 | J Houston | 1745 | J Blake | | |
| 1838 | JG Fawcett | 1948 | W Kiton Davis | | |
| 1690 | J Woodall | 1784 | J Skelton W Hay | | |
| 1861 | H Hassard Short | 1960 | J C L Hawkins | | |
| 1695 | J Ferguson | 1791 | S Drummond | | |
| 1884 | RT Shea | 1977 | C G Elliot-Newman | | |
| 1696 | W Clark | 1987 | F Blanchard | | |
| 1702 | Robinson | 1996 | B Giblin | | |
| 1705 | J Smith | | | | |

*References: Dr D Finlay*
*ed. Martin Dreyer*
*Updated B Lawson 2000*
*Updated R Hughes 2008*

# Chapter 9

# The Chapel

The history of Methodism in the York area dates from about 1735-1740 and the village records indicate loyal support for the Society of Wesleyan Methodists. In July 1759 John Wesley arrived in York to conduct the opening service at the new Peasholme (Aldwark) Chapel and it is almost certain that Stockton's Methodists were present. The Wesleyan faith had many followers here and one can imagine the great man himself walking out to this village to attend a service held in a private house. Perhaps the gathering may have taken place in the open air near a young oak tree at the end of Beanland Lane.

*Stockton House*

Thomas Wilkinson joined the Society about 1760 and did much to ensure the stability of the local group. Members gave generously to the Society sending 13s to the quarter board when Scarborough's contribution was a mere 10s 6d. In 1780 on Lady Day and at Midsummer, Methodists donated £1 1s 6d, the fifth highest sum in the region. Stockton once housed one of the most prominent York Methodists, John Lupton. Born at High Bishopgate, Nidderdale in 1765 and converted to the Methodist faith at Pateley Bridge when 18 years old, John completed his apprenticeship as a linen weaver before moving to York. He eventually entered the service of local preacher Mr John Woodcock who lived in the village. Mr Lupton became a great advocate and leader of Sunday schools, ensuring a basic education for the poorest children, servants and apprentices. In 1791 the first Methodist Sunday School was founded by John Lupton at the Peasholme Chapel. Services were held here every month and it is recorded that Thomas Wilkinson preached on 28 August and 28 October 1792. Thomas Pears conducted the service on 30 September. Monthly services continued but there was no permanent place of worship available at that time.

Thomas Wilkinson's grandson (also Thomas) was a member of the Independent Church in London. He built Stockton House with the intention of living there on occasions with his wife Susannah. Thomas died in 1826 and his wife set up 'The Wilkinson Trust' in May the same year. The document consists of two parts:

1. An endowment of two rooms in a dwelling, Stockton House, Stockton on the Forest. One room was to be used as a schoolroom and the other as a chapel or meeting room for local members of the Wesleyan faith.

2. £166 13s 4d was to be set aside in a bank account and used to administer the said Trust for the benefit of the chapel room.

Susannah Wilkinson nominated specific governors in the Deed Trust, namely J Woodcock, J Hall, Thomas Brown, William Robinson, William Wilkinson, Matthew Nightingale, Mr Burdekin and the Agar family. Ministers were to be of the Wesleyan faith and elected by male and female members over the age of twenty one. Sadly, the Trust did not always run smoothly. From 1844 until 1849 there was much disagreement between Pastor Soper and Minister Pritchett, leaving the village without a minister. There were also problems relating to the chapel, school room and Stockton House itself. Rev Fawcett (vicar of Stockton and related to the Wilkinson family) resided at Stockton House with his mother and fully intended to use it as a parsonage. Many letters passed between him and George Lloyd of Stockton Hall, chairman of the Trust but the chapel continued and in 1884 there were 45 practising Methodists. In the late 1950s, when the chapel had an ever-increasing congregation and there were many problems at Stockton House, it was decided to build a new place of worship. Land was purchased and after much fund-raising the new chapel was officially opened in May 1960.

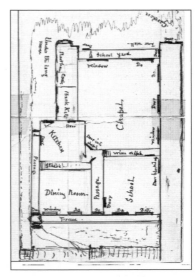

*Stockton House ground floor plan*

## *A personal recollection by Lily Dunn*

*In September 1951 I came to live in the village with my parents. We arrived on the Tuesday and on either Wednesday or Thursday we had a visit from Mrs Worthy who lived where Mr and Mrs Boldry now live. I had received a letter before I came from Rev Clarke, minister at Clifton, who had charge of Stockton telling me something about the Methodist premises. Our minister on the Knaresborough circuit had informed him of our credentials and impending transfer. Mrs Worthy, after welcoming us all, came straight out with her requests: would I undertake to light the stove and clean the chapel and could I play the organ. I soon became aware of the problems and the very small congregation.*

*The first Sunday congregation consisted of Mrs Worthy, George Eden who lived in one of the two cottages near the blacksmith's shop, Mrs Stericker of Rose Cottage, a poor lame gentleman from the cottage next to where the present chapel is and Les Broadley. Mrs Worthy was the only member. The meeting place was a large room lent to the Methodists in the past by someone who must have owned the house. It didn't belong to us - we only had the use of it for worship etc. The question when we arrived was - what was to be done. The house was owned by Arthur (Jack) Broadhead (or perhaps Broadbent, Broadley, Broadhead, or Broadribb). All of these were family names in the village at that time. Part of the house was let as flats. The house was beautifully furnished in the old fashioned way with oak pews all raised up a step. A coke-burning stove was at the front, a large pulpit up several steps, a communion rail, table and lovely kneelers. To one side was the organ with foot pedals and to the other a lectern. There was no cupboard or cloakroom but the cleaning materials and a very small amount of coal for lighting the stove were very carefully concealed in a corner. The coke was kept in a little bunker pushed close to the wall outside.*

Slowly the congregation grew because, as Les Broadley said, the rector at Holy Trinity was not very popular and three or four more came to us. We had a two week visit from Cliff College Trelsius and as a result a Sunday school was begun with help from both local preachers. So we were indeed growing but the premises were hopeless. There was noise from the flat above our heads and from behind the premises. If a preacher parked his car outside the door there would be a knock and a not very pleasant "move that car".

The circuit meeting took over our cause and a committee was formed taking the decision that we would have to move. Having found a plot of land for sale, our minister Rev Nicolas Wells, who followed Rev Clark, was able to help us raise money. We got an interest free loan from an anonymous member of the circuit to purchase the plot. We then set to work fundraising. Mrs Worthy's large lawn gave us room for stalls and soon money began to come in from all around. Mr Ernest Firth, the city architect and a member of Clifton Methodist Chapel, offered to do the architectural work free of charge (except for the expense of plans etc.) and a local preacher solicitor, Mr James Sutcliffe, offered to give his services too.

The new chapel

After only eight years of living in the village we were ready to build a chapel of stone. Who better to lay the first stone than Mr LW Bowman of Bowman's Butchers who had been one of the two acting trustees for the old premises. The other trustee was Mr Wright of Wright's Pork. Children asked their grandparents, aunties etc if they would buy a brick and for each donation they stuck a paper brick on their card. On the stone-laying day each child secured a brick to place on the foundation. A small wall was built and, when I left Stone Riggs in 1999 and moved to Woodhall Spa in Lincolnshire, their initials were still visible. Donations came in, some quite large and many into four figures. Our premises were opened in September 1960, on a pouring wet night. The congregation was so large that the service was relayed to a coach outside. Now we had our own premises. You entered a wide hall with a Ladies and Gents to the right and a vestry. The main hall was to the left with a dividing screen to separate the chapel and Sunday school when required. A fitted kitchen was reached through the Sunday school room. The village joiner, Herbert Broadley, had been commissioned to make the oak pews. Many of the furnishings had been donated with some bearing donors' plates. A pair of brass flower vases stood on the communion table. In centre place there was a wooden font. The woodcarver in Shambles had carved the font from a piece of timber recovered from York Minster when the work of underpinning its foundations took place.

What about the room in the original house? It was no more use to us yet, as J Sutcliffe pointed out, it could become a liability if its neglect caused damage to the main building. It was agreed he should pay a very nominal sum to the owner and so we finished with it. I suspect that legally it wasn't quite as easy as it sounds. The house was at one time owned by Mr Dixon, a schoolmaster. I heard, but cannot verify, that during the war the house had been occupied by the WLA (Women's Land Army). If I remember correctly, the house was next door to the Joiner's shop or very nearby.

The first baptism to be conducted in the present chapel was for the first grandchild of Lesley and Marian Broadley. There should be a register giving names. On 9 December 1967 our wedding was the first one to take place when I, as Lily Cordukes, married Ernest Dunn.

## Recollections by Joan Rawkins

We moved to Stockton on the Forest in 1970 when the present chapel was ten years old. Sunday services were very well attended with many teenagers in the congregation. I don't remember a Sunday school for younger children at the chapel then but I do know there had previously been one. My son remembers going to the Junior Guild at the home of Mrs Bolton for one evening a week. Services were held on Sunday evenings but during the winter months we had afternoon services, changing to the evenings when the clocks changed.

In 1982 Mrs Dunn, our treasurer, explained that our collections were not meeting the quarterly assessment for the circuit and she suggested having coffee days at her home. Despite this, although other people held coffee days too, we were still not raising enough money to cover our commitments. At this point we decided to have a Christmas coffee and mince pie morning to take place in the chapel schoolroom. We started by charging 50p for the coffee and mince pies together with a small entrance fee. We had a cake stall, jams, marmalade and grocery stalls plus fancy gifts and bric-a-brac. Despite having very few members, we raised a great deal of money. As Methodists we don't have raffles or tombolas so we had to work doubly hard. We raised £300 to £500 at each event but continued having small coffee mornings at our homes. By then we had also established regular coffee mornings at the chapel schoolroom. Eventually we charged £1 for coffee and a scone but no longer

Coffee morning stall

charged an admission fee. Members of other chapels in the circuit supported us and more people in the village came along, including our Anglican friends. We owe a great deal to Raymond Carter and Pam Beresford who decorated the interior of the chapel many times and who installed double glazing free of charge. The Wesley Guild had a meeting every Wednesday evening apart from the summer months. Everyone was welcome and people, including many who did not normally attend our chapel, came to hear some excellent speakers, raising a great deal of money for charities both here and abroad.

In 1997 we set up 'Churches Together' where Anglicans and Methodists shared a Sunday morning communion service once a month at the chapel. This was eventually well attended. The joint service in December was always a carol service held in the evening at the parish church and for many years we also sang carols and read lessons at the Fox Inn. We organised prayer lunches about three times a year. Our Anglican friends supplied one course and the Methodists the other. The parish church had a large Christmas tree in the grounds where we all gathered to sing carols. After walking down to the chapel we sang more carols round our lit-up crib, finally retiring to the warm chapel for coffee, mulled wine and mince pies.

Methodist ministers change churches every few years. In my time in the village we had Sister Eileen Wragg, Rev John Jackson, Rev Dr Lawson, Rev David Kinch, Rev David Jones, Rev Ann Vaughan and finally Rev Graham Peaden. After so much hard work by loyal members it is sad that the chapel has had to close as only very few members remained.

## Recollections by Betty Willis

### From the Village Newsletter - Autumn 2010

We celebrated our 50th Anniversary in fine style with a Golden Jubilee Concert given by the St John's Singers from Brigg. The following day we were joined by our friends from the Parish Church for a Service of Thanksgiving presided over by Rev Richard Andrew, tutor in Community Theology at St John's College.

Our joyfulness at these events was tempered by the knowledge that the chapter would be forced to close in the near future as our members are now so very few (and of advancing age!) making it no longer viable. So, after much sorrowful deliberation, it was decided that our last service at the chapel would be on Sunday 10 October 2010, the preacher being Mr David Marwood whom we have welcomed for many years.

## Postscript

The strength shown by chapel members will continue as they meet with friends, join together for services at Holy Trinity Church and even pause a while to discuss events as they pass by the massive oak tree at the end of Beanland Lane.

*Eileen Hill, Kathleen Carter, Edna Nicholls, Joan Rawkins,*
*Kathleen Shilleto, Vic Paylor, Esme Love*

# *Chapter 10*

# *The Bull Centre*

Built by Hull Builders in 1951-2, The Milk Marketing Board Cattle Breeding Centre was situated on the right hand side of the road coming into the village. Two stockman's cottages faced the centre on the opposite side of the road.

The building housed approximately 35 breeding bulls, mainly dairy breeds: Friesian, Ayrshire and Jersey. Beef breeds Hereford and Aberdeen Angus were later joined by the French breeds Charrolais, Simmental and Limousin. These were used for the artificial insemination of cattle on farms. The centre also included a laboratory and offices.

After joining the European Union in the early 1990s, the Milk Marketing Board unfortunately lost its monopoly and reduced the number of its units, forcing the closure of the York site. The stockman's cottages could not be sold commercially as they had an 'agricultural use only' restriction. They were demolished in 1997 and the whole unit, including 14 acres of land, was sold for building purposes. The cottages have been replaced by Poplars Close which consists of five detached properties. The centre has been converted to four properties named The Woodlands. The land has been let to a local farmer.

MMB Fanfaron photographed on his fourteenth birthday in March, with Leslie Beattie who is the head stockman who looks after him. Fanfaron has played a major part in establishing the Limousin breed in this country. He was imported from France as a calf and has spent all of his life at the Burley freezing unit, in the Yorkshire dales, and at York.

Les Beattie has been the stockman at York since 1955, and also helps with the MMB's display cattle at the Royal, Great Yorkshire and Smithfield shows.

*Stockman Les Beattie with Fanfaron*

# Chapter 11

# *Wellies & Watering Cans*

Ken Dean started work in 1957 for Wright & Harris, a local seed and bulb merchant in York. In 1965 he and his wife Margaret decided to start their own garden centre. By March 1966 they had found and moved to the current site at Stockton on the Forest. Ken continued working for Wright & Harris. He also grew and sold vegetables from a shed at the side of their house. In 1967 Ken and Margaret received planning permission from the local council to build their long awaited garden centre. Ken left Wright & Harris in October 1968 and on 7 December Dean's Garden Centre finally opened its doors to the local gardening community.

The original site consisted of a pre-fab building and a 14ft x 60ft glass house. As there were no full time staff at this point, Mr and Mrs Dean ran the business with only casual help. Over the next three years the garden centre grew in popularity with local gardeners and in 1971 two further building developments extended the garden centre by linking the pre-fab building to the old cow shed. The building was extended further in 1973 and a Pratten

*Advert for the opening of Dean's Garden Centre*
*Yorkshire Evening Press Friday - 6 December 1968*

*Dean's Garden Centre – 1970*

*Below: Mr Dean at the front of the Garden Centre - 1968*

*Right: Promotional advert for the opening of a new extension - 1978 Yorkshire Evening Press*

greenhouse was built. By this time several full time staff were employed to help run the business.

After the first 10 years of successful trading, a major extension to the shop replaced several of the older buildings. This was officially opened in June 1978 by Percy Thrower, Britain's first 'celebrity gardener'. There were now 14 members of staff including the Dean's son, Richard.

A further extension was added in 1981 which included an office, staff room and storage area upstairs. The original greenhouse was replaced by a Cambridge model in 1982. Sarah Nursey, Mr and Mrs Dean's younger daughter came to work for the business in 1985. A second site was purchased at Scarborough in February 1986 which officially opened in April the following year. In 1989 Helen Jones, the Dean's elder daughter, came to work full time within the garden centre which meant that the whole family now worked together.

Major re-developments were started at the York garden centre in April 1991 with the opening of new buildings. These included a sales area, houseplant area, covered area and store - all of which make up the site as it is today. In July 'The Bothy' coffee shop was opened. As there was no space left for growing bedding plants and perennials on site, land on Holtby Lane was purchased in August to build a nursery. This site underwent further development in 1992 with the addition of a glasshouse with poly and net tunnels.

After 25 years in business the Deans retired in 1993, leaving the garden centres in the capable hands of their three children, Richard, Helen and Sarah, who still manage the business today. An outdoor seating area and garden were built in 1994 and, due to the increasing popularity of the York coffee shop, its kitchen was extended the following year. In 2008 the York garden centre celebrated its 40th year.

*Dean's Garden Centre – 1981*

*Dean's Garden Centre – 2007*

*Garden Centre - 2010*

Today Deans employs over 95 members of staff in addition to Richard, Helen and Sarah, covering the three sites. There are eight children between the three partners, five of whom are currently working within the business. Over 30 members of staff have worked there for 10 years or more and one member has been employed at the garden centre for over 35 years.

# Chapter 12

# *The Yorkshire Herald*

4      THE YORKSHIRE H

# TWO EXPLORERS IN OUR COUNTRY DISTRICTS

## A Joiner Who Started Life as a Caddy

DON and I met many personalities at Stockton-on-Forest this week —joiners, blacksmiths, farm workers and retired schoolmasters—and it was only natural that their reminiscences should prove both varied and interesting.

Not the least interesting of them all was Mr. Dixon, district councillor, and whom one might describe as the "general factotum" of the village. He has its interests truly at heart and is always ready to further anything which may improve its amenities. He has lived in the village for more than 50 years, and is the retired village schoolmaster.

He is held in high regard by everyone, and is well known in the district.

### Started As A Caddy

HIS close neighbour is Mr. William Broadley, joiner and wheelwright, and also a district councillor. He has lived in the village for 16 years, and in his joiner's shop (which adjoins the village school) to the accompaniment of the noise of sawing wood and the singing of the school children, we learned that he was a native of Ganton and started life as a caddy on Ganton golf course. He caddied for such famous players as Harry Vardon, Willie Park and John Ball.

It was at Dunnington that he served his apprenticeship in the joiner's shop. Subsequently he was six years at the County Waggon Works in York, and for nine years was a foreman employed by York Corporation. During the war he served with the Royal Engineers.

The village, he says, has developed a lot, and there were to-day practically 50 per cent. more houses than when he first came.

The place in fact was becoming more urban every day, and had certainly lost its rural touch of years ago.

With the advent of the motor car much of the wheelwright section has disappeared, but the other section continues to flourish and there is always plenty of work for him to do. He says that at Stockton there is less hardship than in many other villages. There were no empty cottages and no men out of work. Like other villages, however, it was feeling the shortage of labour, and he thought that the sooner there were more cottages for the rural worker the sooner would the problem be solved. It was one of the things that Flaxton Rural Council would have to consider in the very near future. A rural worker could not get a house in the country at a moderate rent in comparison with the wage that he earned. The consequence was that he sought work in the towns to the detriment of the farmer.

### Coaches And Livery

WE left the joiner's shop and called on old John Britton, who for 57 years was coachman and subsequently chauffeur to the late Mr. G. W. Lloyd, of Stockton Hall. John retired only a year ago, and he still goes down to the courtyard to remind him of the days he spent there years ago. He told me that he could remember Coney-street, York, when it was cobbled, and how in his livery he drove the magnificent old coaches with their silver handles. When he first took up employment, Mr. Lloyd was still at Cambridge. His service with the family, therefore, has been long and faithful. He is 80 years old, and is a native of the village.

*Dick Swann, the village blacksmith.*

### Surprise At The Smithy

BY this time we have become rather used to wandering into the village blacksmith's shop to find him with one hand against the bellows deep in conversation with one of his friends. He would then begin to deplore the fact that there was little or nothing for him to do.

But at Stockton-on-Forest we got a surprise. There were signs of great industry as we approached the forge, and there we found Dick Swann busy shoeing. Business seemed to be good.

For nearly 21 years Dick has been the

*This article dates from 1937*

John Britton and Mr. Cleveland.

village smith. Born at Slingsby, he served his apprenticeship at Barton-le-Street.

"Me grandfather and me great-grandfather were blacksmiths before me, so tha' sees we are a blacksmith family," he told me.

For 17 years he was employed by the railway company at Shildon, and in 1916 he came to Stockton-on-Forest. Despite the fact that "times 'as altered," he says there is still plenty of work for him to do particularly as far as implements are concerned, so one presumes that the trade may not die completely.

And then we met Mrs. M. Goodall,

## Darby & Don
### at
## Stockton-on-Forest
## XLV

aged 77, who has lived in the village for nearly 37 years. She lived previously at Newton-on-Ouse and Holtby. Her husband, who died seven years ago, was estate joiner at Brockfield Hall.

In her young days, she was a teacher at Newton-on-Ouse school. She has seen life in the country change almost beyond recognition, but she is one of the few old women who does not regret those changes. There is nothing old-fashioned about Mrs. Goodall. She likes modern ways, modern girls and short skirts. In fact she says that the younger generation "buck her up."

We also met her daughter, Mrs. Scott, with whom she lives. Her husband was killed in the war during service with the East Yorkshire Regiment.

### The Grandson Overseas

MRS. SCOTT'S son, Robert, is in the R.A.F., stationed at Iraq, where he has been for nearly three years. "Grannie" Goodall, like her daughter, is very proud of "Bobby," as they call him, and each fortnight he receives a copy of the "Yorkshire Herald." The sketch by Don of his grandmother should be a pleasant surprise for him. We hope this news from his native Yorkshire will be of comfort to him in

Mrs. M. Goodall, who likes modern life.

a foreign land, and will revive happy memories.

Seventy-year-old Mr. Cleveland, who lives with his two sisters, has been resident in the village for some 50 years. The son of a farmer, he was

Mr. William Broadley, joiner and wheelwright.

born at Huntington. He is also a farm worker to-day, but has little patience with modern methods. Like many other "Owd Stagers," he still thinks that the old-fashioned ways were more thorough. He deplored the fact that the younger men to-day were not taking the same interest in the industry.

He thinks tractors are too expensive, and says "there's nowt like a couple of losses."

Another native of the village is Frederick Hick, aged 73, who has been the gardener at Stockton Hall for nearly 50 years. He is one of the oldest residents. A member of the church choir for more than 50 years, he is also a bellringer. He has seen many changes in the village, and he considers that years ago a more "homely" atmosphere reigned in the country village.

### The Oldest Couple

IN Mr. and Mrs. Len Smith we met the oldest couple in the village. Mrs. Smith, who is 86, was born in the village, while her husband, who is 11 years her junior, was born at Sheriff Hutton.

Mr. Smith is a retired farm worker, and at one time he was also roadman in the district. He ceased work about five years ago.

Of farming, he says that the industry is "nowt so good as it used to be."

For some time now I have been wondering what the present farmer must

Frederick Hick, gardener at Stockton Hall.

think of this repeated condemnation of modern methods and the allegation that farming is not as good as it was. I suppose it is only natural for the older men to think that their way of management was better than that of their successors. The fluctuations of agriculture to-day make the farmer rather doubtful as to the true state of his industry. Don and I have met many farmers. Some of them are glad to be retired, others are still carrying on in the hope that conditions will improve, and others assert that the industry is much better than it used to be.

One thing is certain. In 50 years time the farmer will think 1938 methods similarly old-fashioned.

This was our last interview in the village. Other personalities include Albert Able, threshing machine proprietor, Mr. Wilson, grocer, and Mr. Precious, licensee of the Fox Inn.

I learn that Stockton-on-Forest is to lose its Rector, the Rev. C. Reed, who is to go to Saxton, near Tadcaster.

# Chapter 13

# First Class Service

### Recollections of Life at the Village Post Office
### by Joy Garvie

*The Post Office - circa. 1988*

On 3 November 1987 I moved with my husband Joe to Stockton on the Forest to start our new life running the Post Office and shop. He was to be Postmaster and I would run the shop and newsagents. My eldest daughter was at Lancaster University at the time but we brought my younger daughter Julia and my father with us. It was a very early start as we were moving from Essex and had to collect my father's belongings first before we could start on our own house.

We arrived about 12 o'clock – luckily at the same time as the furniture van. A stock take was in progress in the shop and we only had half an hour to unload before a balance was to take place with the Post Office auditor. That afternoon and evening was spent trying to unpack our boxes and locate where everything was kept in the shop. A late night was had by all. At 5.30am on the next morning we were ready to mark up the paper rounds and meet our paper boys - Simon Rycroft and David and Christopher Jilbert. My husband then went out in the car and delivered to the surrounding areas of Hopgrove and Malton Road. Breakfast was eaten in between serving customers, which was to be the norm for the next thirteen years.

*Christmas 1988*

At 8.45am a training officer arrived from the Post Office. In those days you were only given a week's training and anything you were not sure about had to be looked up in an enormous, confusing manual. Post masters now have far more training and there is also a telephone help-line. While Joe was getting to grips learning his new job, I was learning about different brands of cigarettes and sweets and coping with an old cash register which had seen better days.

The old cigarette machine was on the outside of the shop wall, next to the post box - something which wouldn't be allowed today. The lino on the floor had big holes – a definite safety risk. Dog food was displayed near the sweets! Giving tender loving care was a must and took priority. We were of course also meeting the people of the village which was to be the most important aspect of our lives. We had no training when we took over because the previous post mistress and her husband had both been ill and could not give us the time we needed. The training officer from the Post Office threw out ten bin bags of old forms the first day. The previous owners had only stayed for a year and the business had been neglected.

After our first Christmas we started Sunday paper rounds in Warthill, Brockfield and Holtby and later that year Joe also delivered morning papers to Brockfield and Holtby. We now had four morning rounds plus what we delivered in the car. The Press was printed as an evening paper at this time and six boys and girls were needed for the rounds. The Press started using new machinery soon after we arrived which meant there were a lot of teething troubles. There was breakdown after breakdown; newsboys had to hang around waiting and our telephone was continuously ringing with people demanding to know where their newspaper was.

Our normal day would start at 5.30am. I would mark up the days' papers, hoping all the boys would turn up, then Joe would go off in the car. The shop closed for half an hour and I shot upstairs for a quick shower before opening again for early customers. Next, the teenagers came in before catching the school bus - a very busy chaotic time, followed by children and their mums on their way to the village school. While marking the papers one morning I looked up to find a cow's face pressed against the window. I don't know who was more frightened - the cow or me, perhaps she had run out of milk and knew I sold it at the village shop! Cows were still herded along the village in those days. One Sunday morning I was chasing sheep off the road which had escaped from the field opposite. On another day there was a horse charging down the village without a rider – see what you miss by not getting up early in the morning!

By 8.45am people would already be queuing for the Post Office with pension books and family allowance books at the ready. Mondays and Thursdays were always the busiest days. Having collected their pensions, they came over to me to pay their paper bill. I had an enormous book with about seven hundred pages in - we never did get around to computers! People used the Post Office much more then. Pensions were paid into the Post Office and not into banks and people wrote to each other more often. There were no emails. It was always a lively place where we discussed the weather or listened to people's problems. I was told by a neighbour and customer that I should have been a social worker! The latest scandal was discussed and we put the world to rights. Of course there was always a lot of laughter. Every day we closed for lunch and in the winter we would light a fire and have forty winks. A few times there was a knock on the back door - "Is the Post Office open yet?" Forty winks had turned into forty five!

*The original letter box*

At 3.30pm the younger children came in. This was penny sweet time! All the sweets were kept in a cabinet on the floor. I think I spent more time on my knees than the vicar did! School bus teenagers arrived a bit later to buy crisps, sweets and fizzy drinks and finally the paper girls and boys came in, ready to deliver The Evening Press which had hopefully arrived. As the Post Office got really busy from then on with parcels and last minute mail, I went and delivered the papers in the car. The postman arrived at five o'clock and things would calm down a bit. The Post Office books were balanced, papers and magazines were tied up to be collected in the morning and as six o'clock arrived it was time to cook dinner, providing all the papers had been delivered correctly.

In 1998 we put the Post Office up for sale as my husband had reached retirement age. We showed many people round the property and most fell in love with the house but they weren't interested in the business - too many hours of work maybe. By 2000 we felt that, at our age, 13 years was enough, especially as we hadn't had a proper holiday in all that time. We passed the newspaper business on to the other shop and they applied to run the Post Office. In February 2000 I delivered the last morning newspaper which was the last morning delivery in the village. Although we didn't sell newspapers and magazines, we still ran the shop and Post Office until May when the change took place and the whole business moved to 52 The Village.

# Chapter 14

# Open All Hours

Mr and Mrs Nurse and their two young daughters moved into The Supply Stores at 52 The Village on 2 September 1953. They bought a plot of land and had a purpose-built store with living accommodation which was then one of three shops in the village. It was very different from what we see today, providing counter service rather than self-service. The present day shop uses what was then the garage, store room and a covered passageway.

Mrs Nurse was in charge of the shop with help from Ossie (as he was famously known). Ossie also managed a mobile grocery

*Mrs Nurse in the shop*

*Win and Ossie*

*Lynn and Angela Nurse playing outside the Stores*

round delivering provisions to an area covering Osbaldwick, Heworth, Huntington, Haxby and Wigginton. The shop stocked everything from kindling wood to firelighters, baby feeding bottles to dummies and much more. If an item wasn't in the store, it would be there ready to buy later that day or the next. Sugar, tea and blocks of lard all had to be weighed and wrapped. Time was spent filling the shelves and topping up sweet jars, of which there were many, situated on the shelf across the shop window. Bacon, cooked meats and cheese were all cut to order. Bread was delivered everyday to the premises, except Sunday, from Wray's Bakers in Scarborough, arriving at about 6.30 am. The shop stayed open until 6 pm on weekdays but often, just as they were sitting down to a well earned meal after a hard day, someone would knock at the back door saying they had forgotten something. It was always 'service with a smile'. Company

51

representatives regularly called at the shop to take orders and many an hour was spent discussing stock whilst chatting over a cup of tea and a piece of homemade cake.

The shop closed at 1.00pm on Saturdays. Mrs Nurse and the girls would then fill up the little van with provisions for Ossie's mobile round. Saturday was a very busy day for him and he didn't usually arrive home much before 9.30 pm. While he was out, other chores were done such as cleaning the large fridge and the bacon machine. Shelves also had to be re-stocked ready for another busy week. On Sunday the shop opened between 3.00pm and 5.00pm; this was because a Wall's ice cream freezer had been installed and the company's condition in providing the freezer

*The famous van*

was that the shop must open on Sundays, but only to sell ice cream, sweets and cigarettes.

*Above: The Pensioners January 1961*

*Left: Saturday night dance at the Hopgrove circa 1960*

Ossie was one of the founder members of the Pensioners Group. He organised coach outings, dances at the Hopgrove which he used to MC and ran a weekly whist drive in the village hall on a Monday night. He also organised the annual Christmas dinner. The family ran the shop for 22 years, during which time they led busy and happy lives meeting the needs of the village people and making many friends. Sadly Mr and Mrs Nurse had to retire in December 1975 due to Ossie's ill health. He subsequently died in September 1976, aged 62. Mrs Nurse lived in the village until her death in March 1991, aged 73.

## Chapter 15

# Sup Up Lads!

*"There is nothing which has yet been contrived by man, by which so much happiness is produced, as by a good inn." Dr. Johnson*

Yorkshire folk have long had a reputation for heavy drinking from as far back as the 16th and 17th centuries. Drinking groups were common place for those who could afford it, encouraging a sense of good neighbourliness. Industrious individuals brewed ale for their own benefit before inviting friends and acquaintances to share the ale and then grossly over charging them. From these outlets and social gatherings permanent 'drink houses' or inns were developed. Travellers and visitors were welcome at Stockton inns which have traded here for many years. Stockton has always been a predominantly rural village with an agricultural workforce which enjoyed a drink or two after toiling in the fields, farm, corn mill or blacksmith's shop. Three original establishments are the Fox Inn at the village centre on the main street, the Four Alls situated on the main road to Malton at the edge of the village boundary and the White Swan which is now a private house, just three houses away from the Fox.

## The White Swan

The house was built in 1735 and given to Elizabeth Kershaw along with many acres of land on her marriage to Seth Agar. It was mentioned in records of 1823, pre-dating the Beer House Act of 1830. Tadcaster Tower Brewery turned The White Swan into a public house in 1835. It was given a temporary name of The Rose and Crown in 1884. An upper storey was built to provide living accommodation and the cottages and barn were made into one unit. During the recent refurbishment the wooden gantries on which the beer barrels were tapped in the old cellar were found, albeit in a rotten state. Even after 50 years they still retained the smell of ale when moved. Real ale no doubt!

On 16 January 1884 a director of Tadcaster Breweries visited the pub. He found the tenant, Mrs Metcalf, the worse for drink and managed to persuade her to give up the tenancy. On his return to York he received a message that she had been found dead at the bottom of the staircase.

In later years The White Swan was tenanted by three sisters and a brother named Cleveland. Trade gradually declined and the family finally gave up the licence in 1947. At one time a butcher's shop was attached to the inn.

### NAMES OF LANDLORDS RECORDED AT THE WHITE SWAN:

| | | | |
|---|---|---|---|
| 1823 | Thomas Jebson (victualler) | 1889 | George Cleveland |
| 1872 | Thomas Metcalf (victualler and tailor) | 1904 | Elizabeth Cleveland |
| 1881 | Ann Metcalf | 1921 | Frederick Clench (?) |

## The Four Alls Inn

Situated on the main east coast road to Malton, The Four Alls is on the edge of the Sandburn Estate which comprised between 400 and 500 acres of woodland, arable and pasture land owned by the Duke of Sutherland. Although there are records of The Four Alls in 1872, there is also mention of a Windmill Inn on the Malton Road in 1889. As there was a windmill immediately behind the site occupied by The Four Alls, we can only presume there was a temporary change in the title.

The name 'Four Alls' originated in medieval times when it was thought that the world was divided into four parts chosen by God although the following rhyme gave it a more secular meaning:

*The king who governs all, the parson who prays for all,*
*The soldier who fights for all, the farmer who pays for all!*

Because of the inn's position on a busy coast road, it has attracted the occasional opportunist trying to make a 'bob or two'. One local regular arrived each Sunday in the car park on a bicycle with a small trailer full of freshly cut flowers which he sold to passing tourists. The only problem was his need for regular refreshment. Perhaps trading at an inn wasn't such a good idea as he had to be rescued several times from hedges and ditches on his way home. There would have been little profit for his household at the end of the day.

### NAMES OF LANDLORDS RECORDED AT THE FOUR ALLS:

| 1872 | Thomas Lund | 1901 | Matthew Marriot |
|------|-------------|------|-----------------|
| 1881 | Mary Lund | 1909 | Thomas Lund |
| 1889 | Thomas Smith – Windmill Inn | 1913 | Matthew Marriot |
| 1891 | Henry Kilvington | 1937 | Frank Cole |

## The Fox Inn

Situated in the centre of the village on the main street, The Fox has remained an active trading establishment since first listed in 1823. The name was changed to The Rose and

Crown for a period in 1884. In 1886 an inquest was held at the inn concerning the body of a new-born baby which was found in an adjacent farm pond, covered in paper and with a piece of string tied around its neck.

The original building has been altered and extended several times over the years as a succession of owners and landlords provided different facilities in order to capture the growing drinking and dining trade. The Fox enjoys a long held, respected reputation for hosting local clubs and events. It also offers a convivial atmosphere for meeting friends and neighbours over a drink or a meal.

### NAMES OF LANDLORDS RECORDED AT THE FOX:

| | | | |
|---|---|---|---|
| 1823 | John Heslegrove | 1896 | John Smith |
| 1840 | William Braithwaite | 1896-7 | Slater Blackwell - Ox Inn (?) |
| 1872 | John Hall | 1921 | James McVeighty |
| 1889 | John Reynolds | 1929 | Frederick Cleveland |

As with all village inns The Fox has been the scene of many pranks and much fun, particularly involving young men. The local bobby was always a target and on one occasion he approached The Fox at closing time hoping to catch late drinkers. One local character went quickly out of the back door, ran round to the front and rode off with the policeman's bicycle. The policeman eventually found his bicycle the next day leaning against a tree in a field further down the village. Needless to say, everyone knew who the guilty party was, including the policeman, although he couldn't prove it!

# Chapter 16

# *From Hut to Hall*

*Mrs Cobham, Rev Cobham, Rosemary Lloyd, Cyril Lloyd, Mrs Lloyd, William Broadley, Joe Pulleyn - 1946*

In January 1945 a letter was received by the Parish Council from the Yorkshire Community Council referring to possible village improvements, most particularly for village halls and playing fields. The contents of the letter were duly considered by the council and it was decided to obtain full particulars for further consideration. Books and pamphlets giving more detail were studied and the matter was deferred to a later date. On 12 June a letter was received from the secretary of the Women's Council of Social Services urging them to take action for the provision of a village hall and playing fields. As a result of this letter a special parish meeting was called on 27 June in the village institute. A full and free discussion took place, following which the motion was put forward by Fred Wright and seconded by Mrs Cobham that 'we acquire a village hall'.

The village hall committee was formed from representatives of the British Legion, the National Fire Service, Old Comrades, the Parish Council, the Show Committee, the Women's Institute and the Young Peoples' Association. Their brief was to find a site for village hall and playing fields and report to the parish council. A council meeting was held in January 1946 to discuss progress. Captain Cyril Lloyd was asked to sell some of his land. However, he said that he would donate the land to the village. A village hall support fund was set up. Major and Mrs Teulon donated £200, Fred Wright gave £50 and a garden fete raised £195 14s. At that time a YMCA hut was offered to the village which was sited at Bubwith. Mr Broadley and Mr Pulleyn visited the hut and gave a favourable report. It was offered for sale at £400. The committee decided to purchase this hut on 23 July and it was dismantled, moved and stored until it could be erected on good foundations with a brick wall. It was decided that 'every effort must be made to get it erected before the rain and snow arrive'.

*The first village hall*

At a meeting on 23 January 1947 it was decided to call the building Stockton on the Forest Village Hall. It was opened in February with a dance and whist drive. On 7 February the first annual meeting of the Village Hall Committee was held comprising a committee of 16 people, 75% of whom 'must reside in Stockton'. Weekly film shows were introduced and a dancing club was started for one night a week. Attempts were made to organise a youth club. It was soon realised that the premises were not entirely suitable for a number of reasons and in 1948 plans were made for the enlargement of the building.

An unused hut situated in Stockton Hall Park formed an extension to the existing building. Forms and tables to furnish the hut were bought at a cost of £16. In January 1949 the Infant Welfare Clinic started activities there and the school began using the hall as an overflow classroom facility, despite being a good walk from the main school. The premises were valued in 1949 at £161. It was suggested at the management meeting that, before any new extensions were considered, plans for a tennis court should be the next priority.

It was proposed that a re-building fund should be set up in June 1967 to enable the village to plan for a permanent village hall. It was proposed and accepted that there should be a week long fundraising campaign each year when all organisations using the premises would be asked to participate. A large target thermometer was to be displayed near the present hall showing the current level of donations. Beat dances were planned every fortnight - a major innovation for the village! Weekly bingo sessions were started together with a village lotto club, a village autumn dance, a great bonfire night and sponsored runs. Lots more ideas came flooding in including house-to-house collections, sponsored walks, whist drives and a tote. One significant decision was to introduce a village carnival to be held at the village hall. A separate re-building committee was set up to manage and report on the project.

In November 1967 £51 had been raised but by February 1972 a magnificent total of £5,200 had been achieved, thanks to the hard work of the villagers. It had been noted in 1970 that the outside woodwork of the existing hall was in a very bad condition and a re-build was urgently required. New regulations had been introduced concerning village halls so that more improvements to the existing hall were necessary. There was general agreement in the village that building the new hall had to be started as soon as funds permitted and, under the chairmanship of Mr Cyril Harrison, the project gathered momentum. After agreement had been reached between the committee and a professional design company, a decision was taken to place the order. In August 1972 Reema (Chesterfield) Ltd was contracted to supply and erect the new village hall. Several months later, and after years of planning and hard fund-raising work, the villagers achieved their goal and proudly took possession of a new purpose-built village hall.

*The present village hall*

# Chapter 17

# *Pen, Ink and Blots*

*Old School Building - 1960s*

Stockton was fortunate in benefitting from a most unusual charity, the Wilkinson Trust, in 1826. The benefactor was Mrs Susannah Wilkinson, widow of Thomas Wilkinson. He had built himself a house in the village (the present Stockton House) some time before. The Trust consisted of an endowment of two rooms in a dwelling in Stockton, one part to be used as a schoolroom, 16ft x 14ft, and the other as a chapel. A sum of money was set aside to administer the Trust. However, the schoolroom was for the education of boys only. Girls were not considered to be worth educating. The boys had to be taught reading, writing and arithmetic for five years but they could be dismissed for mis-conduct. Pupils had to be nominated to obtain a free place at the school: two boys by the minister of Stockton Church, four boys by Mrs Susannah Wilkinson (or the occupier of Stockton House), two boys by Benjamin Agar and two boys by Thomas Price of Stockton Hall. The master of the school was to be appointed by the trustees of the charity and he received a salary of ten shillings. The school room and chapel were reached by a right of way from the main village street.

In 1856 the number of scholars increased to 70 and the school room was considered to be too small with concern expressed about the health risk from overcrowding. A new school was provided by Miss Lloyd of Stockton Hall. It was built in a mock tudor style, at her own expense, and provided good rooms and a house for the master. A mistress was also employed. The pupils paid a small sum quarterly except for the ten free scholars. By the 1950s conditions in the school were appalling with overcrowding, inadequate toilet and cloakroom facilities and no school hall. In the 1960s and 70s pupils had to walk a third of a mile at midday, in all weathers, to the village hall for lunch.

Stockton was promised a new 160 place school by North Riding Educational Committee but in 1972 difficulties arose over site access. The new school was eventually opened in 1976. Until the 1960s scholarships were provided for village pupils to help with senior school costs. The Wilkinson Trust continued to be managed by the Kershaw and Lloyd families and the parish council until 1995 when it was finally closed.

## A Teacher's View by Joan Rawkins

*When my husband retired in 1970 we decided to leave London and live closer to my relatives in north Yorkshire. At an interview in Northallerton I was offered two posts, one of them to teach juniors at a village Church of England school at Stockton on the Forest. At this point the interviewing panel seemed very anxious to explain that the old school building was far too small for the number of children and lacked the desired amenities but a new school was to be built shortly. In fact it was six more years before this happened.*

*The old school building was shared by the two classes: the upper juniors and the lower juniors. We had a very heavy wooden screen between the classes. This had to be opened for assembly every morning and closed again at the end. We were joined by the reception class and top juniors who each had a pre-fab in the grounds for their classrooms. Being a Church of England primary school, the rector Rev John Hawkins would frequently come in for morning prayers. At other times the assembly was taken by Mr Smith and we all remember how frequently he chose 'Fight the Good Fight' for the morning hymn. The classrooms of the old school were very dark and we couldn't see out of such high windows. The rooms were heated by old coke-fuelled stoves which were encircled by huge fire guards. Pupils sat two to a desk with little room between them, so children on the back row had to climb over other desks to get to theirs. My first day at school was quite a shock having previously been at a very modern school. This was such a contrast!*

*At lunchtime on the first day the teacher in the adjoining class asked me if I had stoked my boiler. I hadn't realised that I was responsible for it. However, having removed the heavy fireguard, I struggled to lift the coke-filled hod. When I put it on the fire black smoke blew everywhere. Having done this I asked where the staff cloakroom was, only to be told that there wasn't one. We used the children's toilet when they were not there. I then had to put my coat on as we had to walk to the village hall for lunch.*

*Although the school was achieving above average results it was still a 'chalk and talk' system with big blackboards in each class where sums and copy writing were chalked up. The children were learning to read by the ITA system but we had very little in the way of back-up books so we dropped this and it was amazing how easily the children changed over. Art lessons were really difficult. We had two buckets of water to fill jam jars for each desk but because of the over crowding water was spilt all over the place. We did not have anywhere for PE other than the playground which could only be used on dry days. Sports Days were held on a field belonging to Mrs Andrews, a former teacher, although one year we all went by coach to Monk Stray. When it was time for the village carnival, all members of staff helped to decorate the float so that the children could take part in the procession. School numbers continued to grow so we rented the large hall in the new village hall until 4pm each week day during term time. I loved being in the village hall as we could have PE, movement and music, dance, games and dry indoor playtime – indeed everything we could not do in the old school. We had lovely toilets and washing facilities and we did not have to walk from school for school dinners - we simply moved in to the next room.*

*Eventually in 1976 the new school was built. We had a huge playing field, large assembly hall which doubled as a gym and kitchens enabling us to have school dinners cooked on the premises. The staff had a comfortable staff room and good classrooms. At last the headteacher and his secretary both had their own office and the children had good toilets and cloakrooms.*

*Mrs Rawkins with the Reception Class in the New School*

There was a problem with the size of the classrooms as each room was to have a carpeted area with tables and chairs and a wet area with sinks and working surfaces. The architects had to cut a metre from the width of the building and it was taken from the seating areas which, once again, meant overcrowding with tables and chairs in the wet area. In the end one of the pre-fabs was transferred to be alongside the new building and became the classroom for the top juniors. The wet areas in the main building were wonderful for allowing the children to express their creative skills; it was such a change from the old school I came to in 1970.

Despite all the problems, in the 19 years I was teaching there, I cannot imagine being at a happier school with more dedicated teachers.

Mr Smith, who fought so hard for the new school, retired in 1978. At his funeral several years later the first hymn was . . . 'Fight the Good Fight'. The next headteacher was Mr John Faunt who retired in 1988. Mr Stone then became deputy head before Mrs Sheard took over as head later that year.

RONALD Smith, the former headteacher of Stockton-on-the-Forest Primary School, has died aged 81.

Mr Smith died at his home in the Heworth area of York on Monday. He leaves a widow, Joan, and son, Paul.

Mr Smith retired from the Stockton-on-the-Forest school in 1978 after 15 years as head-teacher.

His period in charge saw school numbers double – and the old Victorian building make way for a new, purpose-built school.

**Ronald Smith**

He was a teacher for 35 years and was three times president of the Easingwold Association of the National Union of Teachers.

He was also secretary of Stockton-on-the-Forest Parochial Church Council for 10 years.

A funeral service will be held at Holy Trinity Church, Heworth, on Wednesday, followed by cremation at York Cremato-rium.

*Obituary - Ronald Smith*

## School head says farewell

PUPILS from Stockton on Forest Primary School have said goodbye to their head Mr John Faunt.

Mr Faunt, aged 62, retired after nine years at the village school.

To mark the occasion, staff and pupils presented Mr Faunt and his wife, Pat, with special gifts.

Mr Faunt, a keen art lover, received an oil-painting kit from children.

Staff followed up his interest in local history by presenting him with a book on the dialect and architecture of North Yorkshire.

He also received a photograph album with pictures of everyone at the school. Mrs Faunt, a former teacher, was presented with a basket of flowers.

Mr Faunt, of Aspin Lane, Knaresborough, thanked everyone for their gifts.

PUPIL Natalie Chambers presents Mrs Pat Faunt with flowers while Greg Evans Matty Dale and Robyne Fletcher present Mr Faunt with his gifts. Picture: George Hendrie.

## *A pupil's view 1938 - 1945*

When I was five years old I started at Stockton on the Forest school just like the children of Hopgrove do today. My elder sister had been at the school for three years before I started so I was used to going there with my mother to collect her. It is about two miles from Hopgrove to Stockton, making a round trip of four miles each day. On the first day my mother took me on a seat at the back of her bicycle. My family didn't own a car, not many families did, and there were no buses on that route. Sometimes we would go along Malton Road and cut across Sowray's Trod but usually we went along Stockton Lane.

The old school building was brick built with a high sloping roof. Attached to the side was the headteacher's house and the toilets were outside and round the back. In front of the school was a playground made of dirt and ash surrounded by a 3ft high brick wall. Inside there were two classrooms divided by a sliding screen. The windows were high in the wall so there was no chance of looking out at the view. To keep the classrooms warm in winter they were provided with two 'pot bellied' stoves protected by a surrounding metal railing guard. These could get very hot turning bright red if they were burning well. One of the classrooms was for the infants and the other for juniors. There were only two teachers – Miss Dalby and the headteacher who I remember was called Miss Wray. All the children sat at desks with a tip-up seat and a top in which to keep books. We sat in rows facing the teacher's desk and a blackboard.

*Miss Dalby with some of her pupils*

62

Lessons were very simple. I remember we did a lot of copy writing and sums from the blackboard. In the infants I remember using a slate and pencil to write but in the juniors we had a scratchy nib pen and a bottle of ink that smudged everything. Paper was expensive and because of the war we had to be careful not to waste it. The books we had to read were very boring and didn't have many pictures. However, I remember how much I looked forward to the teacher's daily reading of adventure story books. Several times a week we would sing songs at the piano. Some afternoons when the weather was fine the boys went to weed and sow seeds in the teacher's garden while the girls stayed inside and learned to sew. Next to the school was a joiner and cart maker called Broadley. I remember leaning over the wall in summer watching the men making carts and fitting hoops on to the wheels.

During the war we each had a bottle of milk at morning break and our dinner was cooked at Strensall Army Camp and brought to the school in heated tins. The Second World War lasted throughout my schooldays at Stockton and had an influence on them in many ways. Airfields and army camps were dotted around the countryside near the village. We saw lots of soldiers and army vehicles - sometimes tanks. There was a camp next to Stockton Hall and I remember the soldiers throwing a party for the children and how we were given rides around the field in army jeeps. In case the children needed protection from bombing raids we practised walking to Stockton Hall and going down into the cellars underneath. The Hopgrove public house cellars were also used as a possible shelter. Quite a few bombs were dropped round the villages, especially during the raid on York when the railway station was badly damaged. We watched the aircraft during the attack from our house in Hopgrove.

My sister and I joined the Stockton church choir when I was nine though I didn't stay long before joining the Methodist Sunday School which met in the chapel down the side of Stockton House (105 The Village). I remember the front part of the house was a Land Army Girls hostel at that time and sometimes 'slide shows' (Lantern Lectures) were held there. The Sunday school had some special outings to the Hermitage on Malton Road where we rowed a boat on the lake and had a picnic. At the end of the war our family moved into York.

# Chapter 18

# Carnival Time

*A local group with their version of 'Ye Old Toy Shoppe' - 1969*

During a meeting of the village hall management committee in 1968 the question of a new village hall was raised. The old one was very small, wooden and definitely needed replacing. Tom Game had the brainwave of holding a carnival – little did he know then what he had started. The first meeting was held on 19 March presided over by Tom Game, John Hornby as secretary with H Stimson, C Murfit, L Marshall, B Aket, Mrs Waghorn, Mrs Lee, Mrs Coulson, Mrs B Hardisty, Mrs Crossley and Mrs Finnie as committee members. It was agreed to hold the first carnival beginning 1 June and finishing on 8 June 1968.

*The Minstrels and an unknown rider during the first carnival parade - 1968*

## The first week's programme in 1968 ran as follows:

**Saturday 1 June:**
8.00 pm Grand opening dance with buffet and bar
Election of Carnival Queen: Cost 9/6d inc buffet

**Sunday 2 June:**
2 pm Parish Ladies v Parish Gents cricket match on Stockton Hall School grounds
Admission free. Collection

**Monday 3 June:**
10.30am Six a side comic polo match on bicycles behind the village hall
11.15am  Pram races from Stockton Hall to The Fox Inn
2.00 - 4.30pm Childrens sports, PE display – Stockton Hall grounds. Collection
7.30pm Super bingo at the village hall - Admission Adults 1/6d

**Tuesday 4 June:**
7.30pm: Variety show: banjo club, village players, magician, Stockton Hall boys choir
Admission Adults 4/-  Children and OAPs 2/-

**Wednesday 5 June:**
Children's pet show behind the village hall. Admission 6d plus 6d  per pet
7.30pm WI open night with tea, biscuits and entertainment - Admission free

**Thursday: 6 June:**
7.30pm Giant Whist Drive - Admission 2/6  - many fine prizes

**Friday 7 June:**
7.30pm Variety show, cast as before with village school children's choir
Admission as before

**Saturday 8 June:**
GRAND CARNIVAL PARADE
with floats, decorated vehicles, fancy dress, dressed up animals, cycles and band etc.
Route: Hopgrove Hotel car park, Hopgrove Lane, through village turning at Midgeley's Garage,
ending up at village hall. Judging and awards of prizes etc.
8.00pm: TRAMPS BALL: (dress optional) with celebrity tramp!

**Sunday 9 June:**
6.30pm United Service at Holy Trinity Church

For the next two years the carnival remained as a full week of fun and games when the villagers' feet never touched the ground.

On 7 December 1970 the carnival committee met to arrange events for the following year. At that time the fund had achieved the grand sum of £3,279 (£4,000 had been the original target) and the format was changed to a four day event from 28 to 31 May starting with a Grand Carnival Dance

*The Ladies Football team, 1970*

and finishing with the carnival procession on the Monday afternoon, followed by a Roman Orgy in the village hall at night. In 1973 it changed once again to a mini-weekend of events. This consisted of a junior disco talent show with tombola stall, side shows and a beetle drive in the evening (admission 15p). On Monday a carnival procession started from the village hall, through the main street, Stone Riggs, Kingsmoor Road and ended at Stockon Hall.

Children's sports were planned complete with sideshows and stalls followed at 7.45pm by prize bingo and tote double draw in the village hall.

In the mid 70s it became more difficult to get helpers to organise and man the parade and people who were interested in running the stalls. The village hall had been completed and opened and at a village hall

*Above: The Girl Guides' rendition of 'Box of Tricks' - 1971*

*Left: The Roaring Twenties and The Can Can Girls - 1973*

management committee meeting it was decided that it might be a good idea to run the carnival every other year.

From 1981 a Gala Day and Carnival was organised once again but this time by members of Holy Trinity Church for church funds. It was only for a day but was often opened by local celebrities such as two players from the York City Football Club and a Radio York personality.

## Stockton-on-Forest & Hopgrove

## Carnival & Gala Day 86

in aid of Church Funds

## Saturday 5th July

* ATTRACTIONS *

RAILWAY INSTITUTE GOLDEN BAND
RADIO YORK
FANCY DRESS COMPETITIONS 0-7 : 7-11 : 11-16 years
ARMY STATIC DISPLAY
"EASY RIDER MOTORCYCLES"
RAFFLE : STALLS : SIDE SHOWS
CARNIVAL PARADE with prizes for best floats
Cream Teas and Ice Creams

## Stockton-on-Forest CARNIVAL & GALA DAY

### Saturday 7th July 1984

*Attractions*

**Two Bands**
**Railway Institute & RAF Cadets**
GYMNASTIC DISPLAY
FANCY DRESS COMPETITIONS
0-7 years        7-11 years        11-16 years

**POLICE STATIC DISPLAY**
Raffle ★ Tombola ★ Stalls Galore

BEAT THE GOALIE —
YORK CITY FOOTBALL PLAYERS

*EASY RIDER MOTORCYCLES*

Carnival Parade with Prizes for best floats

WORKSHOPS FOR THE BLIND
Basket making in action
— basket work to buy

**SIDE SHOWS**

Cream Teas ★ Hot Dogs ★ Ice Creams

*Two programmes from the 80s show the type of fun and games everybody enjoyed*

*The Best Kept Front Garden competition had started, sponsored by the parish council*

*Below: The Parade - 1985*

The carnival continued with Bryan Lawson at the helm for about ten years, until 1998 when he handed over the reins and resigned as chair of the carnival committee.

*Holy Trinity Church Choir 'Masters of Mirth' - 1985*

Other types of entertainment like Karate exhibitions were also introduced. Stockton Hall always made the carnival a special day, but by the end of the 90s the village hall became the final destination with Stockton Hall as the starting point.

*Above: The Carnival King and Queen: Oliver Hadja and Alison Manners - 1994*

*Left: The Carnival King and Queen: John Bond and Lynsay Ray - 1996*

*By kind permission of The Press*

In 1997, despite poor weather, the carnival once again proved to be a happy event. The village hall was packed with people who were entertained by the City of York Pipe Band, the Market Weighton Square Dancers, Boxo the Clown and the locally based Spicy Girls. There were not as many floats but walking floats became more popular.

*Above: The City of York Pipe Band - 1997*

*Left: The Toddler group stepping out*

*Below left: 101 Dalmations The Brownies - 2001*

*Below: The Vikings are coming! - 2001*

*Carnival Queen Alexandra Spratt and attendants*
*Lucy Acklam and Maya Blakeway - 2002*

*Friday evening entertainment*
*York Quintessence - 2005*

Many people ran the carnival successfully over the years and in 2003 Jill Hawkins decided to extend the event and, with the help of Jean Broadbent, she included a Flower Festival. Jill also organised a Murder Mystery Evening as well as an entertainment in the church on the Friday evening. Songs of Praise was re-introduced to complete the weekend's events. The first Flower Festival had a theme of Blooms, Brides and Baptisms and was very well received. The church always looked wonderful.

*Left: The first Flower Festival - 2003*

*Below: The ever popular plant stall*

The Saturday parade travelled from Stockton Hall to the rear of the village hall. Gazebos and stalls covered the petanque terrains where there was always something for everyone including a roundabout and swings for the children. There were competitions and displays, children's paintings and photography plus tombolas of all kinds. There was even a magician and a juggler.

The carnival was a wonderful village tradition. The history of Stockton's carnival shows it to have been a happy and well supported community event and will be remembered with great affection for many years to come.

# Chapter 19

# Three Cheers For The WI

The WI dates from 1897 and was originally founded in Canada. The movement in Great Britain was not established until 1915. Its aims were to encourage women to become more involved in food production during the First World War, whilst men were away fighting, and to help revitalise rural communities. 'Jerusalem' was first sung at the Annual General Meeting in 1924 and remains the WI anthem to this day. Although not always sung at local meetings, due to a shortage of pianists, it is always included at larger gatherings. Resolutions of national importance have been discussed at the AGMs and put forward to the Government of the day. Many resolutions have been adopted by Parliament but in 1939 the subject of equal pay for equal work became law after 30 years' effort. A resolution passed in 1950 resulted in the national 'Keep Britain Tidy' campaign.

1939 saw the WI helping to organise the evacuation of children from cities. In 1940 The National Federation of Women's Institutes adopted the Ministry of Food's Fruit Preservation Scheme. Three years later Mrs Churchill asked for coats, waistcoats, hoods and caps lined with rabbit fur to be made for the people of Russia and following a huge response 2,071 garments were sent.

## The First Meetings

Stockton on the Forest WI was formed in 1941. Mrs Cobham, the rector's wife, was elected as the first president by the committee of Mrs Abel, Mrs Barker, Miss Broadley, Mrs Cleary, Mrs Cobham, Mrs Cusworth, Mrs Kirk, Mrs Megginson, Mrs Pulleyn, Mrs Fleury-Teulon and Miss Wilson. Miss Pears and Mrs Pickering were co-opted later to represent Hopgrove. Meetings were held in the schoolroom but later changed to the 'Little Institute'. The group met there until 1947 when they moved to the new village hall. A committee was formed to participate in the Co-operative Jam Making Scheme. Sugar could be obtained specifically for jam making and, between 1941 and 1943, 744 lbs were made. Jam making continued until the end of the war although there are no details about the final amount. The total for all WIs combined was 12 million lbs of fruit being made into jam, bottled or canned. Stockton on the Forest jam was made in Mrs Pearson's kitchen on primus stoves. At one time the women worked in shifts from 2pm to 5pm and from 5pm to 8pm. Jars had to be sterilised and properly labelled. Fruit was used in season and children were paid 3d for each lb of blackberries picked and taken to the jam making centre. WIs all over the country were asked to collect rose hips for their vitamin C content and 2/- a stone was paid. Stockton on the Forest WI collected 2 stone and although they did get paid eventually, it took a few months for the money to come through. In May 1942 nettles were the main crop required - not a very pleasant task to collect as leaves had to be stripped from the stalks. The Government asked the National Federation of WIs to collect five tons of herbs and each Institute should provide 2lbs each of mint, parsley, sage, thyme and marjoram. They were also asked to collect foxglove seeds (digitalis) for medicinal purposes.

However, it was not all jam making and herb collecting. Speakers came to each meeting and gave talks on many diverse subjects ranging from glove making to make-do and mend. Even venereal disease was discussed! Bus outings were arranged to local beauty spots and theatre trips were a great favourite. An outing to the pantomime at Leeds each year was well supported. Produce shows were arranged to which the whole community contributed. Whist drives were held to support various causes. The Sunshine Home for Blind Babies, the

National Institute for the Blind, the RNLI and the County Hospital were just a few organisations supported by the devotion of WI members. Queen Charlotte's Hospital, a maternity hospital, requested help as it had been bombed three times and money was raised for the Red Cross by donating a penny a week. Collections were made for Wings for Victory, Warship Week and a house-to-house collection was organised in 1956 for aid to Hungary after the Russian invasion. Fund-raising for charities and WI funds continued for many years, financed mainly by whist drives. These stopped in 1963 and were replaced by coffee evenings which ended when the WI became a charity and therefore had to abide by the rules of the Charity Commission.

## The Arts

From its beginning the WI was involved in drama activities. Haxby and Wigginton WI, formed in 1921, appeared at the First National Drama Festival in London in 1928. Stockton on the Forest WI became interested in drama in 1941 and a drama group was set up the following year. They entered many competitions until the early 1960s, usually with great success and won many awards with very high marks. The pantomimes started in the 60s, and were performed in the village hall, as well as touring round five or six local villages. Eventually the WI drama group opened its membership more widely and was re-named The Stockton Foresters.

*Back row:*
*Mrs Hick, Mrs Pickering, Netta Cusworth, Ann Megginson and Esther Stabler*

*Front row:*
*Pam Thompson, Eve Brick, Mary Pulleyn, Kath Horsley and Ettie Stabler*

In 1948 folk dancing became popular with dancers entering WI competitions very successfully for many years. The group won many first class awards and in 1952 gained 92 points out of a hundred. They were presented with a cup as overall winners of the advanced class. After further success in 1956, the group was awarded the Intermediate Shield with a score of 90 out of a hundred. The last mention in the records came in 1961 when two teams performed at Harrogate and both won First Class awards. The photograph above probably shows the 1956 winning team.

72

*A rail outing to Kings Lynn - 1968*

*Nancy Gifford, Gladys Broadley, Jean Marshall,*
*Phyllis Broadley and Sylvia Finney*

During the 1960s money was still being raised for charity and WI funds from whist drives, coffee mornings, fairs, beetle drives, carol singing and even stalls at The Hopgrove Inn. Items made at the Blind School in York were brought to the village hall once a year and sold at a special 'Blind Sale'. Outings and theatre visits were arranged and were very well supported. Many members attended a wide variety of courses at evening classes to learn about dressmaking, lampshade making and cake decoration.

The WI celebrated its Golden Jubilee in 1965. Mrs Gass, as the Stockton on the Forest representative, attended a Garden Party at Buckingham Palace. Five members attended an International Garden Party at Hovingham Hall and two members sang in the 'Peasants Cantata' at Harewood House.

The WI has always supported events in the village. In 1968 it was proposed that a new village hall should be built and the WI was heavily involved in fundraising. The proceeds of a whist drive were donated to the re-building fund, food was provided for the carnival dance, rosettes were made for the carnival and the sash was made for the carnival queen. Valerie Crossley produced a musical show together with a float and walking group which were entered in the Carnival Parade. Morris dancers processed from The Hopgrove Inn to Midgley's Garage and back to Stockton Hall.

*Carnival Floats*

*Above: 1968*

*Left: 1969*

1970 saw the Golden Jubilee of the Yorkshire Federation. To mark the occasion members agreed to erect a seat outside the village hall. They also presented the primary school with two cups for the top boy and girl in the school sports. It was also proposed to plant some trees at the village hall but this was deferred until the new building had been completed.

The archive records only go as far back as 1974 - information about the missing records would be welcome. The photographs below show birthday celebrations over the years. In 2011 we are celebrating 70 years of the Women's Institute in Stockton on the Forest.

Stockton on Forest W.I. last night presented two silver cups to celebrate the Yorkshire Federation's jubilee year, to Mrs. M. A. Andrews (right) a teacher at the village school. They are to be competed for annually and go to the best boy and the best girl in sport. The presentation was made by the W.I. president Mrs. M. Cleary (on left of picture).

*40 Years*

*Back Row: Mrs Sellers, Miss Broadley, Mrs Pulleyn, Mrs Musson, Mrs Cusworth,*
*Seated: Mrs Cleary, Mrs Pickering*

*50 Years*

*Mrs Brick, Mrs Pickering, Mrs Pulleyn, Miss Broadley, Mrs Musson*

*60 Years*

*Back row: Dorothy Buckton, Mary Watkinson, Sylvia Finnie, Kitty Crossley, Barbara Hardisty, Edna Game, Margaret Sherry, Joy Garvie, Pauline Hebditch, Phyllis Broadley, Phyllis Wilson, Jean Marshall, Beryl Boyce, Pam Brighton, Jenny Stanley, Gill Tipping, Macy Ford*

*Front row: Shirley Gill, Edith Musson, Mary Pulleyn*

# Chapter 20

# *Treading The Boards*

*Above: Jill Hawkins, Malcolm Jennings, Jane Palmer and Betty Midgeley*

*Right: The Crypt - 1944*

Stockton on the Forest Women's Institute was founded in 1941 and soon afterwards the vicar's wife, Mrs Cobham, began a drama section. In 1943 Mrs Cleary had entered them in the WI Drama Eisteddfod, their performance earning 73 points out of 100. Under the leadership of Mrs Fleury-Teulon the group won a first class certificate for their production of 'The Crypt' in 1944, later adding the Shakespeare Cup to their collection. Naturally the company was made up of women with an occasional male guest appearance.

Although the repertoire ranged from Shakespeare to pantomime, it was the panto which eventually took centre stage under the care of Hettie Stabler. By the 1960s Kitty

Crossley was in charge producing the annual pantomime which consumed the village for months. The cast performed to full houses for the entire week.

This original group was so popular that productions were taken 'on tour' to local villages. The conditions were truly primitive as stages were created from planks on bales of straw. The cast often had to crawl off stage behind a suspended blanket and sometimes they fell off if their dancing was too enthusiastic. Health & Safety legislation sadly put an end to these tours.

*Pat Hawksby, Jill Hawkins, Pat Jennings and Bryan Lawson in 'Aladdin'*

In the early 1960s new housing which had been built in the village brought an influx of younger families and they joined in the pantomimes with enthusiasm. One newcomer, Pat Jennings, who was an ex-drama teacher entered the group in the Choral Verse Speaking class at the WI Drama Festival. Reminiscent of Mrs Fleury-Teulon's days, the group won the silver cup for best overall performance. Pat began expanding the repertoire again, complementing the pantomime, in conjunction with the WI but with a wider community membership. For a year or two this arrangement continued but, as the majority of members were not in the WI, the organisation was seen to be un-workable. There was an amicable agreement to separate the drama section which then became an all-inclusive village group.

This was the period when villagers were busily fund raising to build a new village hall. The old hall was not only very small and cramped but the stage was little more than a platform, hazardously reached by steep steps. There were no 'wings' and only a tiny

*'Stepping Out': Jill Hawkins, Shirley Kilshaw, — , Debbie Nicholson, Pat Jennings*

*Jill Hawkins, Paul Arrowsmith, Eileen Maidment, Daniel Twiddy, John Piercy, Malcolm Jennings*

communal changing area. It was a miracle how the WI producers managed to organise 24 performers on stage, including a high kicking chorus line. Naturally the drama group members were amongst the most enthusiastic fund raisers, helping to design the new hall with a much larger stage and 'wings' with separate changing rooms.

Stockton Hall Community School provided a valuable and talented resource of male actors. One of the first recruits was young actor John Hall. He was soon sharing the producer's role with Pat Jennings and they continued in an almost unbroken partnership for many years. Their repertoire ranged from serious drama to farce, from full scale musicals to musical reviews, from classical playwrights to new and even local ones. More recently new members have, in turn, taken on the task of directing, thereby giving the group fresh impetus.

Over the years several members have organised charity fund raising events and have also written murder mysteries which continue to be popular, raising thousands of pounds for local charities. An annual 'soiree' for more serious singers and readers has been organised by Jill Hawkins (a previous pantomime principal boy).

The less formal seating arrangement used for the 'soirees' with the audience seated cabaret-style around tables rather than in rows, proved to be so successful that it was adopted for the main shows and is still used to this day. Table centre pieces are themed to the production and waitress served refreshments are provided in the interval together with a wine and juice bar. The ambience is unique to this group and is greatly appreciated by the audience; every show is a sell-out.

The group has a strong sense of fellowship with an active and happy social side to meetings. Much fun and laughter accompany the hard work of rehearsing and planning. One memorable event happened in the 1970s. While dress rehearsing 'The Rape of the Belt', set in ancient Greece, the police arrived to collect the York Coroner who was dressed in a very short Greek tunic and the Deputy Principal of Stockton Hall who was clad in a bear skin, wielding a cave man's club. Both were required urgently for their official duties. One can only wonder what the miscreants thought!

*Rebecca Williams, Jane Palmer, Pat Jennings, John Hall, Aubrey Houlden in 'An Inspector Calls'*

The group's long running success can be attributed to its community involvement. The Stockton Foresters, despite its popularity well beyond the immediate area, remains a village organisation. The present chairman, Mary Coulson, is still a WI member and is a former pantomime belle. Members have presented concerts and entertainment in various village locations: in the church and pub as well as in the village hall. They augment the church choir at festivals and take part in the village carnival. Their riotous carol singing in the village pub each Christmas always starts the season with a swing. Drama group members can also be found in other village groups: the WI, the Church, the Brownies, the Gardening Club, the Petanque and Cricket Clubs, the History Group and the Village Hall Management Team. They even meet up on the village golf course. The Stockton Foresters not only perform to a high standard but they are also well integrated into village life. Let's hope it remains so for another 70 years.

# Chapter 21

# *Musical Folk*

*Brian Oxberry, Steve Marshall, Dee Marshall, John Hall, Rhona Hall, Fred Ring , Jim Boldry*

When John Hall came to live in Stockton on the Forest in 1970 he needed help to tune a guitar which he'd bought. Susan Boldry told him that her husband Jim played the violin and might be able to help; in fact the violin had been banished to the attic because Susan hated it! Jim wasn't able to help with the guitar but meeting John and sharing his enthusiasm meant that the violin saw daylight again after 14 years. On 5 November 1971 they gave their first performance at the Scout Group Bonfire Party. Regular sessions began and Derek Mortimer joined with a banjo he had inherited. Derek's brother, Noel, contributed a tea chest and broomstick bass to form a skiffle group called The Deep Litter Boys whilst John and Jim played at the church carol service as Carol Medleymania.

The group's first booking was in a wooden pre-fab grandly called the village hall and which was destined to become the first Dean's Garden Centre. The WI had invited them and a grand total of £38 was raised for the RNLI. The group soon grew as Rhona, John's wife, and Brian Oxberry, his work colleague from Stockton Hall School, joined - adding their talents and widening the repertoire. Their style of folk, skiffle and country music was heavily influenced by The Dubliners, The Yetties and Steeleye Span. They became known as 'The Foresters' and performed in various venues from Butcher Terrace to The Lowther, The Old Britannia Inn, The Bonding Warehouse and The Barge - which sank under the strain!

Having been bitten by the acting bug John and Rhona left to focus on drama. Steve and Dee Marshall, Fred Ring and later Mike Brown had all guested with the group so often that they became permanent members. They played residencies at The Hopgrove, The Black Bull, The Corn Mill, The Highwayman at Sheriff Hutton, The Squirrels, The Black Swan, The Fox at Upper Poppleton, The Tanglewood, The Four Alls, The Bay Horse, The Derwent Arms at Osbaldwick and, for a whole season, The Tilly Morrison Bar in The Spa at Bridlington. Several Parent Teacher Associations invited The Foresters to play annually at school events. The narrow folk repertoire was broadened to appeal to a wider audience. The group appeared on the Harry Secombe TV show 'Highway' and were filmed playing on the revolving turntable of the National Railway Museum. They also performed in the Museum Gardens after the Mystery Plays, assisted by the hand of God (John Hall) and a noble chieftain (Brian Oxberry).

Bookings arrived twice in 1984 for the TV programme 'Saturday Superstore' and for Radio 2, Radio York, Radio Hull and Pennine Radio. The Foresters played a memorable concert as support group to George Melly and his band at The Assembly Rooms. A concert for the Fire Brigade at The Viking Hotel was interrupted when the candles on a cake triggered the smoke alarms and the whole hotel, with many of the guests in night attire, had to evacuate to the street below - in freezing conditions!

A concert at The Merchant Taylors' Hall was abandoned when the River Foss flooded the premises. On another occasion a very attentive audience at Bridlington Spa was actually looking past the group through a bay window to watch the lifeboat rescuing the crew of a sinking yacht. It was noted at the

*From the cover of their album 'The Foresters'*

group's 30th anniversary that they had raised well into six figures for various charities. Fundraising has continued over the last ten years including annual concerts for Macmillan Nurses and St Leonard's Hospice. Over £1,000 was raised for the Cystic Fibrosis Trust at a concert in the De Grey Rooms. The Foresters' concert in the village hall for the Haiti disaster appeal raised nearly £2,000.

*Rhona, Brian, John, Jim - 1971*

*Dee, Brian, Mike, Steve, Fred, Jim*

# Chapter 22

# *Sporting Times*

Many English villages have shown an enthusiastic involvement with sporting activities and Stockton has been no exception. Over the years there has been a village bowling green, tennis and badminton clubs at the village hall and a very keen soccer team. However, the true criterion for a Yorkshire sporting village is to have a cricket team made up from local players.

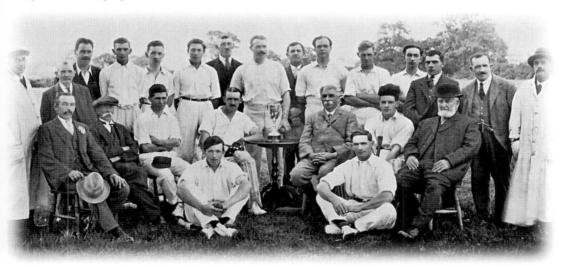

In 1933 the cricket authorities formed the York Saturday League. The Stockton team joined after the war but the early post war years showed a decline in the number of cricket teams. National Service, the war itself and the need for working men to concentrate on earning a living, all contributed towards a general loss of interest. During these hard times Stockton farmers, landowners and other interested benefactors were approached for financial help. Wives and girlfriends helped to raise funds by providing refreshments at the annual dance in the village hall. Cricket club subscriptions were initially set at 2s 6d per year.

Stockton and Hopgrove Cricket Club was set up in 1948 as a result of a merger between the Stockton on the Forest and Hopgrove Clubs. This was a sensible move as Stockton had

*Winners of the Prendergast Cup at Dringhouses - 1947*
*Back row: Roy Charlesworth, Frank Greatham, --, --,*
*Ron Atkinson, Jack Watt   Middle row: Fred Allen,*
*Bob Suttle (wicketkeeper), Fred Sellers (captain),*
*Fred Wragg, Tony Rogbe, Doug Betts*
*Front row: Tom Sellers, Mary Watt (scorer), Jack Ross*

only £19 in the bank and Hopgrove's assets were reduced to a bat and two pairs of pads. The quartet of Fred Allen, Tom Smith, Les Pears and Fred Sellers formed the new club which has been in existence for more than 50 years and which is still going strong. The club still continues its policy of using local players.

*Stockton and Hopgrove Cricket Club*
*Winners of the Dr Riddolls Cup at New Earswick - 29 July 1951*

*Back row: Roy Charlesworth (umpire), Ron Atkinson, Laurie Cooper, —,*
*Tom Sellars, Dr Riddolls, Brian Watt, Jack Ross (umpire)*

*Front row: Fred Allen, Fred Wragg, Frank Greatham, Doug Betts, Fred Sellars*

The team regularly played on land to the rear of the village hall. Unfortunately on one occasion a gate was left open and several cattle escaped. It was time for the team to look for a new home. During the 1950s the club moved to the Knavesmire and played most of its games there until the 1970s. In October 2000 work started on the cricket square at the new Hopgrove Playing Fields Association site on Malton Road. This continues to be the home ground for the Stockton team.

*The Cricket Club Dinner and Dance - 1952*

Tony Kerrison has been a quality batsman for the cricket club since making his debut in 1958 and has enjoyed playing alongside brother Robin and sons Richard and David. Tony has probably been the club's star player and has scored over 30,000 runs. Long serving medium pacer Nigel Collinson has also achieved a club record of 2,000 wickets during a long career. There have been several other cricketing families notably Roy Charlesworth with his son Alan and Fred Sellers with his son Barry.

The team has had great success entering for many cups, especially the Prendergast Cup where they were winners in 1948, 1959, 1972, 1977, 1979, 1986 and 1987. They were also winners of the HPH Cup in 1997, 2001 and 2002. They won the Prendergast Memorial Trophy in 1998 as well as winning the Evening League in 2002 and 2003.

*Above: Stockton Football Team 1978*
*Right: Stockton Football Team 1979*

In 1978 the village formed a football team to play in the York and District Sunday League and competed successfully for many years under the name of Stockton Fox. Later this team was joined by a second eleven who competed in a lower division. The Stockton Juniors were formed in 1984 and competed successfully in the Minor League for four years coached by Noel Marshall, supported by Brian Lawson as secretary and with valuable help from parents. Many of these players progressed to the adult Sunday League team. The pitch was situated for many years on the corner of Norgat Lane but in 1998 the club was allowed to play at the back of Stockton Hall. When this field was needed for building development the seniors moved to Low Moor in York and the juniors, on completion of their four years in York and District Junior Leagues, were absorbed into the seniors.

The sports teams have been fully supported by Denby Hawkins who has devoted many hours of work as player, groundsman for 30 years and representative on Ryedale Sports Council, as well as taking on many other duties. He is ably assisted by willing volunteers and even equipment repairs can be made in-house.

Alan Jackson, former Fox landlord, decided to make use of the unused buildings to the rear of the pub by creating the Sports Bar. Here darts and dominoes were played and village sports such as the new football team and the long established cricket team could hold their meetings. In 1998 David Halliday, landlord, had the initiative to set up a Petanque club behind The Fox. There has been so much interest in Petanque that a permanent floodlit area and club house have now been built behind the village hall. The team has enjoyed much success, travelling and playing away matches in north and west Yorkshire.

*Stockton on the Forest Bowls Team at Journey's End - circa. 1952*

*Vince Compton, Bob Tarbotton,*
*Sid Southernwood, Frank Brighton,*
*Frank Coates, Ted Brighton,*
*Harold Simpson, Charlie Colville*

*Petanque Team at their new home*

# Chapter 23

# *Tally Ho!*

*Lord Halifax and the Middleton Hunt - 1950s*

The hunting of animals has always played an important part in English country life, providing employment, food and sport and also the necessary control over animal numbers. The Forest of Galtres was home for many animals and birds and was famous for the quality of wild boars. It has been suggested that York's name originated from Eborwic (Ebor: a wild boar, wic: a refuge). The earliest recorded foxhunt with hounds in Britain dates from 1534. By the late 19th century fox hunting was at its most popular. An increasing number of the middle classes improved their social standing and ensured that fox hunting activities continued to grow. Fox hunting and hare coursing have long been established in the area to the east of York. Foxhounds owned by Sir Marcus Sykes were active here in 1812 and the forest remained a favourite spot for his successor Sir Tatton Sykes in 1840.

George Lloyd of Stockton Hall was one of the best known huntsman of his day and a thoroughly English gentleman. Most of his hunting was carried out as Master of the York & Ainsty Hunt in 1823 which did not, however, cover the Stockton area.

On one occasion the Bramham Hunt pursued a fox for 17 miles. It swam across the rivers Ouse and Foss before the kill was finally made at Stockton Hall. Mr Lloyd ran out of his house exclaiming "Where did these hounds come from? They are not mine". Details of Lord Middleton's Hunt at Claxton Hall in the 1870s are recorded as meeting at Sand Hutton and running through Sandburn woods. From the early 1900s they met at Brockfield Hall and at Four Milestone to draw the areas of Strensall Common and Stockton Forest. The Middleton Hunt met occasionally at Stockton favouring Turker's Wood and Breck's Wood. This has now ended due to the close proximity of the A64 road.

The village has seen several hunting personalities in its midst. Besides George Lloyd there was Major Teulon and Major General Ward-Harrison who were both leading local huntsmen. Tony Morris, the York Coroner, kept a pack of beagles close by. Even the vicar was seen 'riding to hounds' when Rev Brendan Giblin stabled his horse at Hazelbush House. There is a report of the Hunt chasing a fox into a shed at the back of The White Swan where paint was being stored for re-decoration. One can imagine the chaos of 26 excited hounds in a small space full of paint pots!

One young village farmer who still lives in the village was ploughing a field near Carlton Farm when he

*Tony Morris with Lord Halifax*

was disturbed by the Hunt in full cry. The excitement got the better of him and he abandoned his tractor to follow the hounds on foot. Some hours later he returned to face his irate father as he'd left the tractor engine running!

# Chapter 24

# "All change! Warthill for Stockton on Forest"

The station at Stockton on the Forest was built on the York-Beverley line which eventually formed part of the direct rail link between York and Hull. However, for much of its life the station was known as Warthill. For a branch line of its type, it saw a variety of locomotives including some experimental ones. A petrol-electric railcar prototype was tested on the line during the 1920s, as was the Kitson-Still steam locomotive during the 1930s. In 1953 the first 'continental-style' lifting barriers in Britain were fitted to the level crossing here. Dr Beeching closed the line in the 1960s despite the fact that a modernisation plan had started a few years before and was well on the way to making the line profitable. The line played a major part in the economic and social life of the communities it passed through.

*Warthill station looking eastwards - mid 1950s*

## The Early Days

The story of the line begins in the midst of railway mania with the 'Railway King' George Hudson and his York and North Midland Railway (YNMR). At the age of 15 an inheritance made Hudson one of the richest men in the city. His wealth opened the door to a successful business life and on 21 June 1836, at a meeting to found the YNMR, he became the chairman. George Townsend Andrews was another significant figure. He trained as an architect and came to York in 1825. Andrews designed all the buildings for the YNMR from August 1839 until early 1849, including the first York station in 1841.

By 1845 the YNMR had a near monopoly of railways in the North East. In 1846 Parliament passed the York and North Midland Railway (East Riding branches) No. 2 Railway Act, authorising the railway from Bootham (on the York-Scarborough line) to Beverley (on the Hull-Scarborough line). Work began on 12 August 1846 staking out the part of the line between Bootham and Market Weighton and on 4 October 1847 a service started between York and Market Weighton. On completion the line had stations at Huntington, Stockton, Gate Helmsley, Stamford Bridge, Fangfoss, Pocklington, Burnby and Shipton. Londesborough Park, just west of Shipton, was George Hudson's private station. When he saw the smoke from a train he would ride his horse down a two mile long avenue of trees which linked his home at Londesborough Hall with the station. Ironically the line was later to play a part in Hudson's downfall. In 1846, as an MP and Lord Mayor of York, he had purchased the Manor of Weighton and the Londesborough Estates to add to other lands he owned in Huntington and Shipton. The large profits and compensation claims he made from the sale of this land to the YNMR started the doubts and enquiries that ended his railway career and made him bankrupt.

On 15 September 1847 the railway line through the parish of Stockton was described thus: 'next Stockton (now Barr) Lane is crossed, being approached by a slight curve, the line running on the level: and at the point where it crosses the road from Helmsley to Stockton being nearly 6 miles from York the Stockton station is erected, at about ¼ mile from that village. Here will be coal depots and villages of Holtby, Sand Hutton, Warthill etc. will more or less participate in the advantages resulting from this station'. The ¼ mile to the village must have been an under-estimate as Kelly's Directory was still quoting ¾ mile until 1925, stating that the station was a lonely place on a common with nothing but a rectory for company. It is only in recent times that the village has finally reached the station.

As early as 1849 it was clear that this branch was pointless without the connection to Beverley but it was 1860 before the North Eastern Railway (NER) decided to build this extension. The through line to Hull finally opened on 1 May 1865. Unfortunately many passengers confused Stockton with Stockton on Tees and so in 1867 the station was re-named as Stockton Forest and again in 1870 as Stockton on Forest. On 1 February 1872 the name was finally changed to Warthill.

*Warthill Station in the mid 1950s*

## Bricks and Mortar

There was a level crossing at the York end of the station and the signal box along with the main station buildings were on the Down (from York) side. Passengers crossed at the level crossing to simple waiting accommodation on the Up platform. At some time the station was provided with paraffin lamps which gave a dim light. They were still in use in the 1950s. The main rail crossover lay between the two outlets to the goods facilities. There was a small yard with two sidings, one up to the loading dock and the other to the sack shed where all the grain was stored. Further down was a ramp up to the coal drops or cells and long sidings faced away from the station where goods wagons and trains could be shunted. Burton & Son built the station buildings and stationmaster's house to Andrews' standard design; the main part being a reasonably well-appointed two storey house with the main frontage to the road. The central entrance, which was emphasised by a bold sandstone door case, provided both public and private use. The domestic accommodation was spacious without being unduly large by the standards of the time. The office occupied the platform end of the ground floor, with a cantered bay window giving the stationmaster a view along both tracks. A short one storey office range or waiting room extended behind and along the platform. All water was drawn by hand pump from a well. Two staff cottages were built along side the Up line for the use of railway personnel.

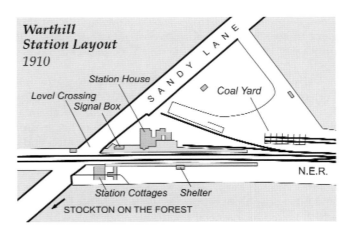

Warthill
Station Layout
1910

Station House
Level Crossing
Signal Box
Coal Yard
SANDY LANE
N.E.R.
Station Cottages    Shelter
STOCKTON ON THE FOREST

90

In 1939 Henry Elsworth arrived from Harrogate to take over as Station Master. He stayed until 1956. Living conditions at Warthill were more primitive than his previous semi-detached home. There was no indoor toilet and washing had to be done in a copper in one of the outhouses. There was a scullery outside in the backyard where the washing up was done and it is believed there was a bath upstairs. Any hot water came from the kitchen range. In 1947 facilities at the station were modernised. Birch's (the builders) put a septic tank in the goods yard providing indoor sanitation. A kitchen was built for the first time in what had been the scullery, so ending the chore of washing up outside.

Holtby station was situated further down the line just before the 90ft. high viaduct at Stamford Bridge. It is the only large viaduct in the East Riding and is still standing today.

*Maurice Emberson and David Clark admiring the flowers at Warthill station - mid 1950s*

## Potatoes and Petunias

In 1895 the directors of the NER introduced a competition and awarded prizes for the Best Kept Wayside Stations to encourage station staff to plant gardens. In 1911 Warthill received a Beginners Class award and a prize of £5. In 1912 they received a Third Class award and a prize of £2 and in 1913 a Second Class award and a prize of £3. The event was not run during the war years. However in 1921 staff again received a Beginners Class award and a prize of £5. We know from photographs there were still patches of garden during the 1950s but whether the staff had any other success is unknown. Goods traffic was seasonal due to the agricultural nature of the area. The main crops were grain, potatoes, carrots and sugar beet which required a daily beet train to be run at the height of the season. Carrot production increased after the Second World War with Warthill, Market Weighton and

Fangfoss providing the major loads. At peak harvest time the express from Hull to York would stop to pick up loaded carrot vans, many of which went on to Glasgow. During the 1940s and 50s 'shoddy' from the West Riding woollen mills was unloaded for farmers at Warthill and, as well as cattle, horse boxes were regularly parked at the loading dock.

## Sand Hutton Light Railway

In November 1919 Sir Robert Walker of Sand Hutton Hall applied to the Light Railway Commissioners to create a railway from Warthill to Bossall. He had built a 15 inch gauge railway on his estate at Sand Hutton prior to the First World War and realised the benefit to his tenant farmers. Work started at Warthill in May 1920 on the 18 inch gauge Sand Hutton Light Railway (SHLR) and by 3 April 1922 it was open to goods traffic from Kissthorn and Claxton Brick Works. The rest of the line was finished by December 1923 and a Saturday only passenger service ran from 4 October 1924.

The SHLR approached Warthill station having travelled down the bridal path by Forest Farm from Sand Hutton. The line crossed Warthill Road (Common Lane) near a level crossing. A single track fanned out into three lines: two goods sidings (one on a raised brick loading ramp) and the third taking passengers to the terminus behind the main line station. Between the high and low level sidings the NER provided a standard gauge siding situated to make easy transference of goods between standard and narrow gauge wagons. All classes of goods could easily be passed down from one wagon to another by manual labour. In July 1927, to assist the transhipment of bricks from the Claxton Brickworks, the LNER installed a mechanical system which straddled the high level siding. It was supported on runners allowing it to be moved along the length of the ramp. Its lifting tackle was capable of lifting one ton and could be moved transversely over both standard and narrow gauge wagons. The only SHLR building at Warthill was a small wooden hut which housed the mechanism of their six ton rail weighbridge.

Passenger services stopped on 5 July 1930 and the line was officially closed on 30 June 1932. While it may have provided a valuable service at first, the line's existence was threatened even before 1919 when it was first envisaged. In the same year, the local National Farmers Union had begun to organise transport by lorry directly from farm to market.

## Re-grouping

At the same time as the SHLR was being built, a major change was taking place in the railway world. On 19 August 1921 The Railway Act was passed providing for the 123 separate railway companies to be grouped into four main companies. This came into force on 1 January 1923 and the NER became one of over 30 component parts of the London and North Eastern Railway (LNER).

## Local news

The station was extremely busy during the Second World War. Major cuts were made to all passenger services to assist the war effort, reducing the timetable to only six trains each way on the line. There were many additional goods and military trains moving between York and Hull. At this time there were two signalmen - Herbert Stones and Bill Clark. Henry Elsworth was the Chief of the Home Guard and their 'dug out' was near the siding buffers. Part of Henry's railway work outside the station was to inspect the Warthill Road/Common Lane and Barr Lane level crossings. During the war he did this on his bicycle even when it was snowing. The Halls were the crossing keepers at Warthill Road.

Wartime winters were harsh with heavy falls of snow. The snowplough train was employed on these occasions which, to the despair of Henry's son Michael, meant that he would be able to get to school. For ten years he travelled to Pocklington on the train with three or four others from York. Delays during the war years meant long cold waits at

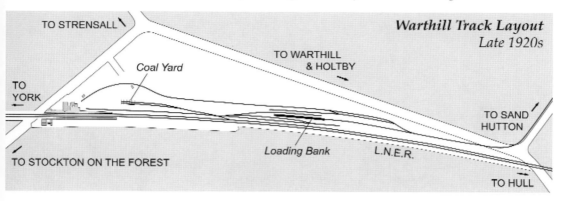

Pocklington station but life wasn't always so grim for Michael and his friends. They had large open areas to play in. At one time Italian prisoners of war worked at the station. He remembers they were wonderful people to have around and they sometimes played football with the boys in the snow. During the summer they played cricket in the goods yard. Occasionally Herbert Stones would come between train times and bowl a few balls. Herbert was a big man and quite a character on the cricket field. He was the only man who had ever hit a cricket ball for six right over the road and into Swann's pond.

Besides being stationmaster Henry also ran the coal business. Customers would collect their coal from the bunkers where the trains came up the incline, opened up underneath and dumped their coal into coal cells. During the war lumps of coal seemed to be disappearing from the cells, so Henry and Herbert Stones stayed up one night and they discovered that the head ganger from one of the staff cottages was stealing coal; he was soon dismissed. The Weigh House where the coal was weighed still stands.

## Crossings

The line crossed many roads and tracks in the 21 miles between York and Market Weighton and there were over 20 level crossings. Before 1851 there was no system of control at these crossings allowing animals and people to stray onto the tracks. Following the death of John Nicholson (a carter who fell asleep on the line while in charge of his ass and cart) it was decided that gates should be kept shut across the road and only opened on request. A simple signal was installed to warn of approaching trains.

In early 1953 the North Eastern Region substituted two 30ft. experimental continental-style lifting barriers for the four 15ft. level crossing gates. These barriers were intended to reduce the heavy maintenance costs of a mechanically operated crossing. This was the first such installation in the UK and why Warthill was given this honour remains a mystery. The station staff always maintained it was because Herbert Stones regularly used to forget the last train of the day!

## Change and Decay

At a half yearly meeting of the YNMR on 6 September 1849 a shareholder remarked that the York-Market Weighton line was *"a beautifully made line but unfortunately without passengers to travel on it"*. The station was nearly a mile from the village. A bus service to York had been started by Mr Thompson of Holtby Lane in the late 1920s and was continued by the West Yorkshire Road Car Company Ltd. With the growth of car ownership after the Second World War it was perhaps not a surprise when on Saturday 3 January 1959 the station was finally closed to passenger traffic.

*Warthill level crossing viewed from the Down platform in the mid 1950s*

As a result of Dr Beeching's infamous report 'The Re-shaping of British Railways', issued on 27 March 1963, goods services finished at Warthill on 7 June 1965 and the station was permanently closed. Saturday 27 November 1965 was the last day of operation on the line and all services were returned to steam haulage for the day. The very last passenger train was a wreath-clad six-car DMU packed with locals and enthusiasts which left York at 9.42pm. Mr L C Sands, chairman of the East Riding Public Transport Development Council, which had fought long and hard to prevent the closure, described the reception at Pocklington as more of a grand opening than an ending. The train's arrival had been announced by the ringing of a hand bell, an old YNMR custom, and over 100 pupils from Pocklington School came to pay their last respects. To the sounds of cheers and detonators cracking the train disappeared into a snow blizzard and the darkness. The service should have ended on 8 October but additional time was given to the local bus companies for new services to be arranged. These included the provision of a York to Hull express coach which was a condition of the line's closure.

The Eastern Railway Board allowed decay and vandalism to take over. Only in early 1970 was the track lifted and buildings demolished or sold. Warthill station was converted into a dwelling. The signal box became a garage and has recently been converted and extended to make a modern dwelling. It is not known when the large extension to the back of the station building was constructed but it does keep faithfully to the YNMR style.

Mr Ken Collinson, who was a signalman at the time of closure, purchased one of the staff houses and some land for a garden. The Up line passenger shelter was on part of this land and he planned to turn the shelter into a summerhouse. British Railways foiled this plan by knocking the shelter down. They did however leave Ken with the substantial brick and concrete foundations, which remain to this day.

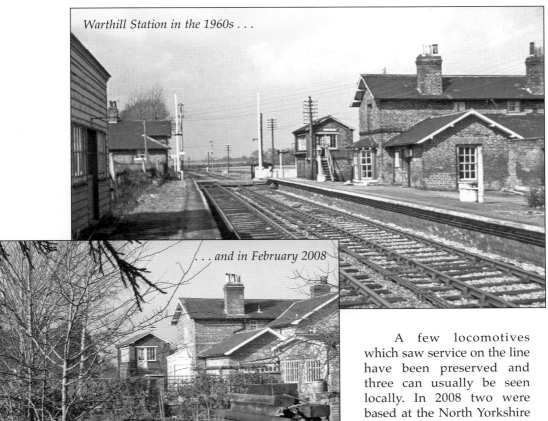

*Warthill Station in the 1960s . . .*

*. . . and in February 2008*

A few locomotives which saw service on the line have been preserved and three can usually be seen locally. In 2008 two were based at the North Yorkshire Moors Railway although not available to view. Class K1 2-6-0 No. 62005 has been on loan to other lines. The boiler ticket for P3 0-6-0 No. 2392 (formerly J27 No. 65894) expired and she is on loan to Darlington as a static display. X2 2-2-4 T66 'Aerolite' is on permanent display in the National Railway Museum at York.

Photo of the station in the 1960s by C.R. Evers used with kind permission of Rosemary Hoppitt.

Charles Wood and Peter Bacon also contributed to this chapter.

# Chapter 25

# Duckhams and Swanns

## Recollections by Frank Swann

### On the buses

The first type of bus we used to go to York on was owned by Farmer Fred Wilson. He had a horse-drawn wagon with a hen hut and seats down the sides. It used to go to York on Market Day. Those who went did their business in York and at a certain time he used to meet you and bring you back to Stockton. I never saw it happen but only know by being told about it. Then, after motorisation came, another chap called Herbert Thompson, who had a

D & R Wallis of York - June 2000

farm up Holtby Lane, he got a motor wagon and put a hut on it and ran a bus route round the area. I've only been told about this by my mother. The first buses I remember were the West Yorkshire - the Red Buses that ran through the village. They went as far as Claxton and came back.

### Blacksmith's Garage

My father was born in Slingsby and then his father and mother went up into Durham to Shildon. My grandfather was a blacksmith and my father was still at school. They came back from Shildon to Stockton in 1914 to take over the blacksmith business of my grandfather's brother, who was called Bell.

From what I've been told, there were two if not three generations of Bells running the blacksmith's shop in Stockton before my grandad took over in 1914. My grandmother was a Bell. My dad came and joined his grandfather and the shop was run as a blacksmith's right up until it was made into a garage.

All I wanted to do when I left school was to be a tractor driver and my mother said to me "If you want to drive them, then you should learn how to mend them and then you can drive _and_ mend them". So I went to Bushell's and mended everything; they even had a blacksmith's shop. My dad and grandad did not want me to work in the blacksmith's shop at home and I used to spend a fair lot of my time at Bushell's.

The property next door to where my mother was born, Westfield Farm, was Alderson's. That's where the chimney is and they used to boil up bones to get the tallow to make candles. That's what my mother told us. When my mother and father got married they wanted a house so they bought two acres of land off a relation called Bell and built 'Pond View' where my nephew Malcolm lives now. His mother lives next door and then my brother and I are on the other side of the field. So we live on 'Swann's Patch', the piece of land my father bought years ago. We all share it now and it joins up with the Blacksmith's Garage.

*Sign on the wall at Blacksmith's Garage*

# Chapter 26

# History In The Making

Beavers - 2011

Cubs - 2011

*Brownies - 2011*

*Scouts - 2011*

*Parent and Toddler Group - 2011*

*School classroom - 2011*

*Parish Council - 2011*                                        *Petanque Team - 2011*

*Stockton Foresters Drama Group - 2011*

*Parish Chuch Council - 2011*

*Stockton on the Forest and Hopgrove Cricketers - 2010*

*Village Hall Management Committee - 2011*

*Senior Citizens Group - 2011*

*Gardening Club - 2011*

*History Group - 2011*

# *Financial Contributions*

*The History Group is most grateful to the following people who have generously supported the publication of this book with financial assistance, without which we would not have been able to proceed:*

*Stockton on the Forest Parish Council  ·  York City Council - Strensall Ward*

*Terry Briggs  ·  Steve Burton  ·  Janet Cockerill  ·  Maureen Cooper*

*Carol Danby  ·  Joy Garvie  ·  Bobby Hughes  ·  Jane Hunt  ·  Malcolm Jennings*

*Noel Marshall  ·  Joy and Simon Moseley  ·  Liz Roberts  ·  Eileen Sharples*

*John Strong  ·  Maureen Sutcliffe  ·  David Williams*